Native American Adult Coloring Book

This Coloring book belongs to:

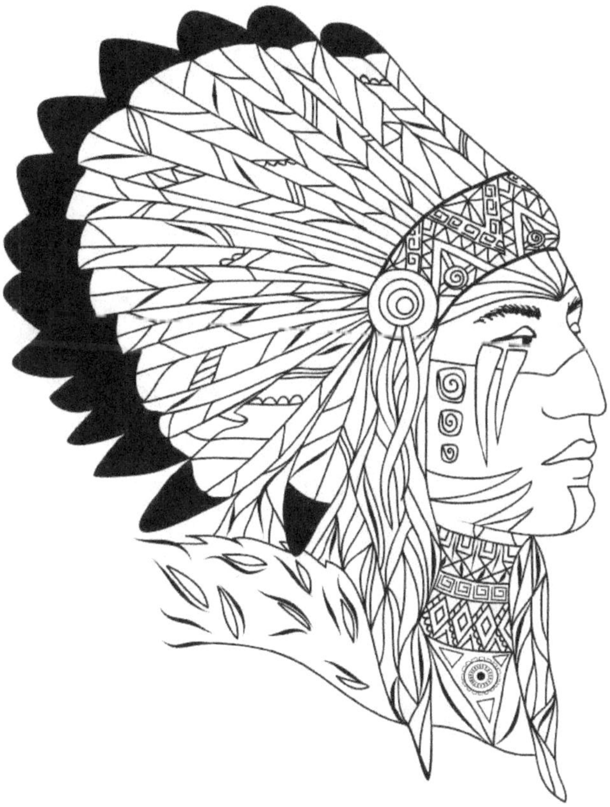

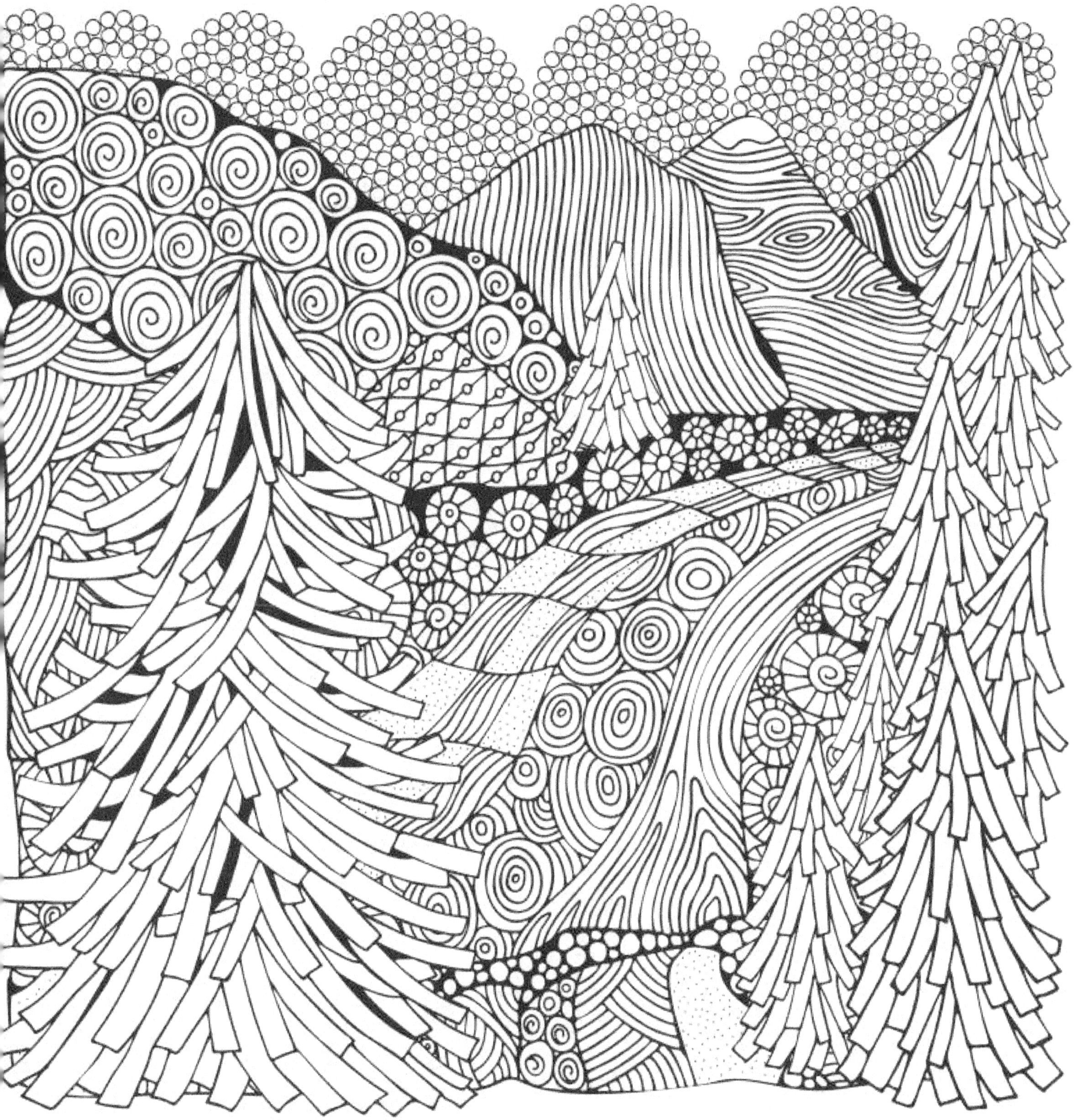

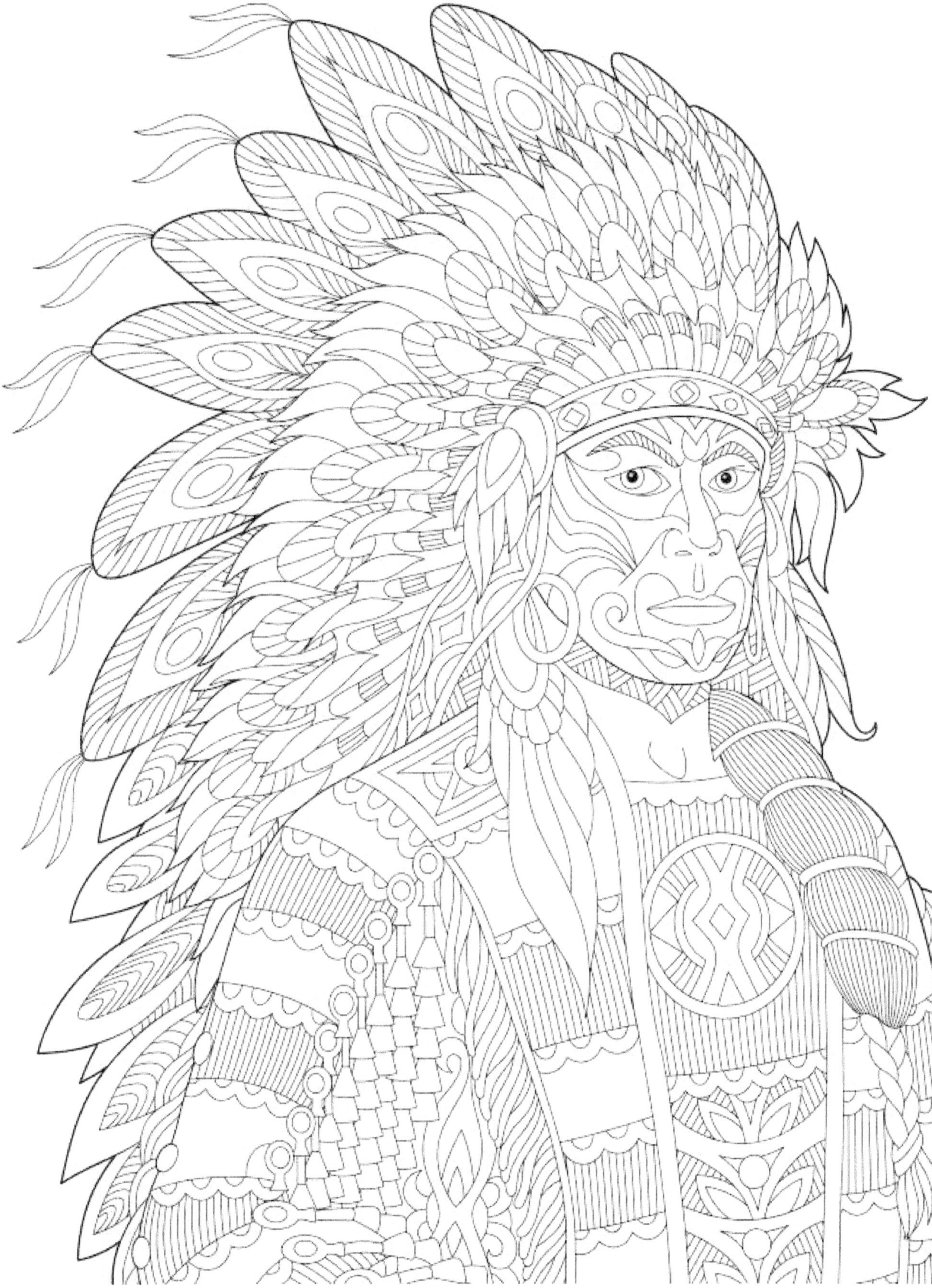

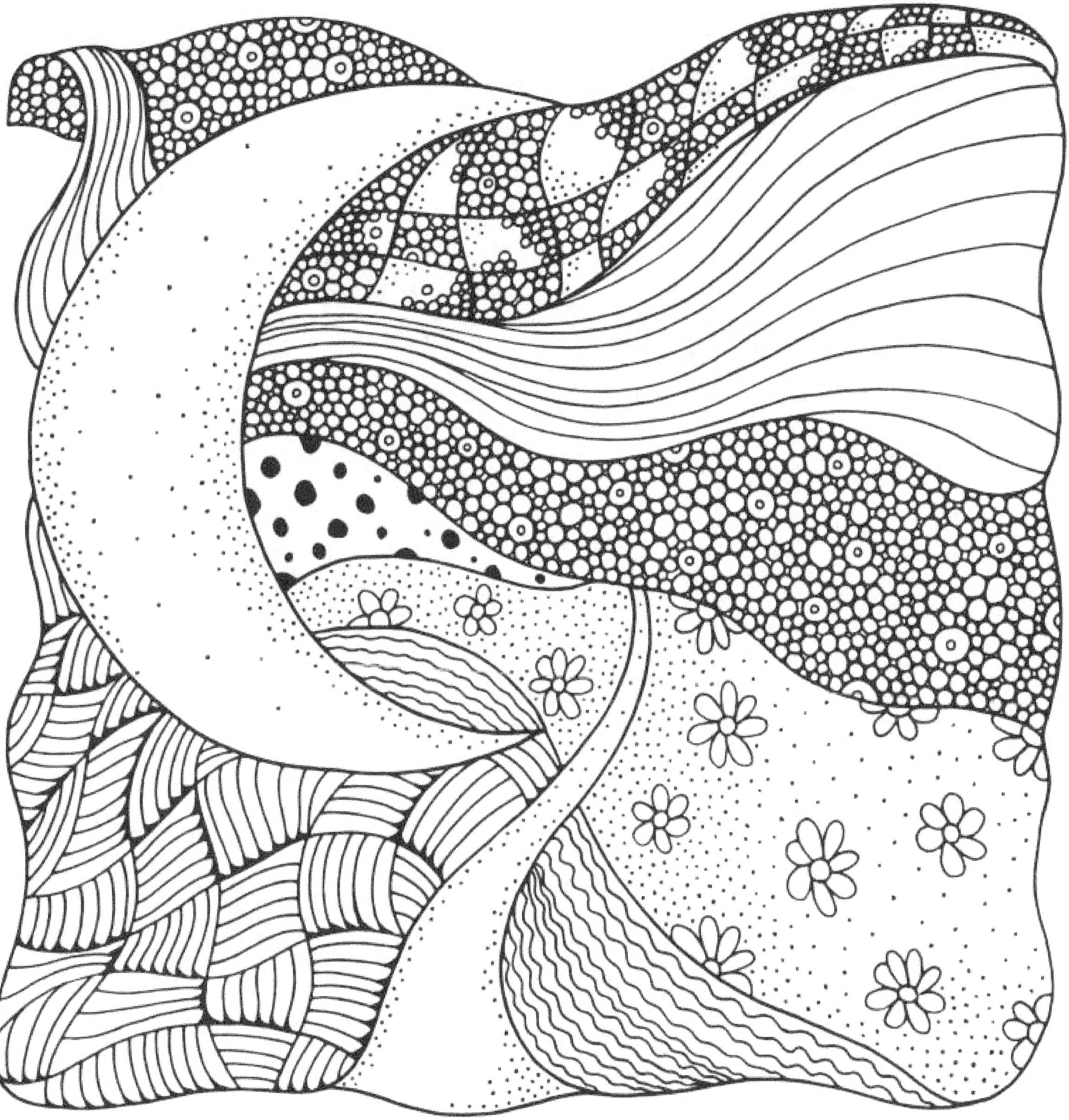

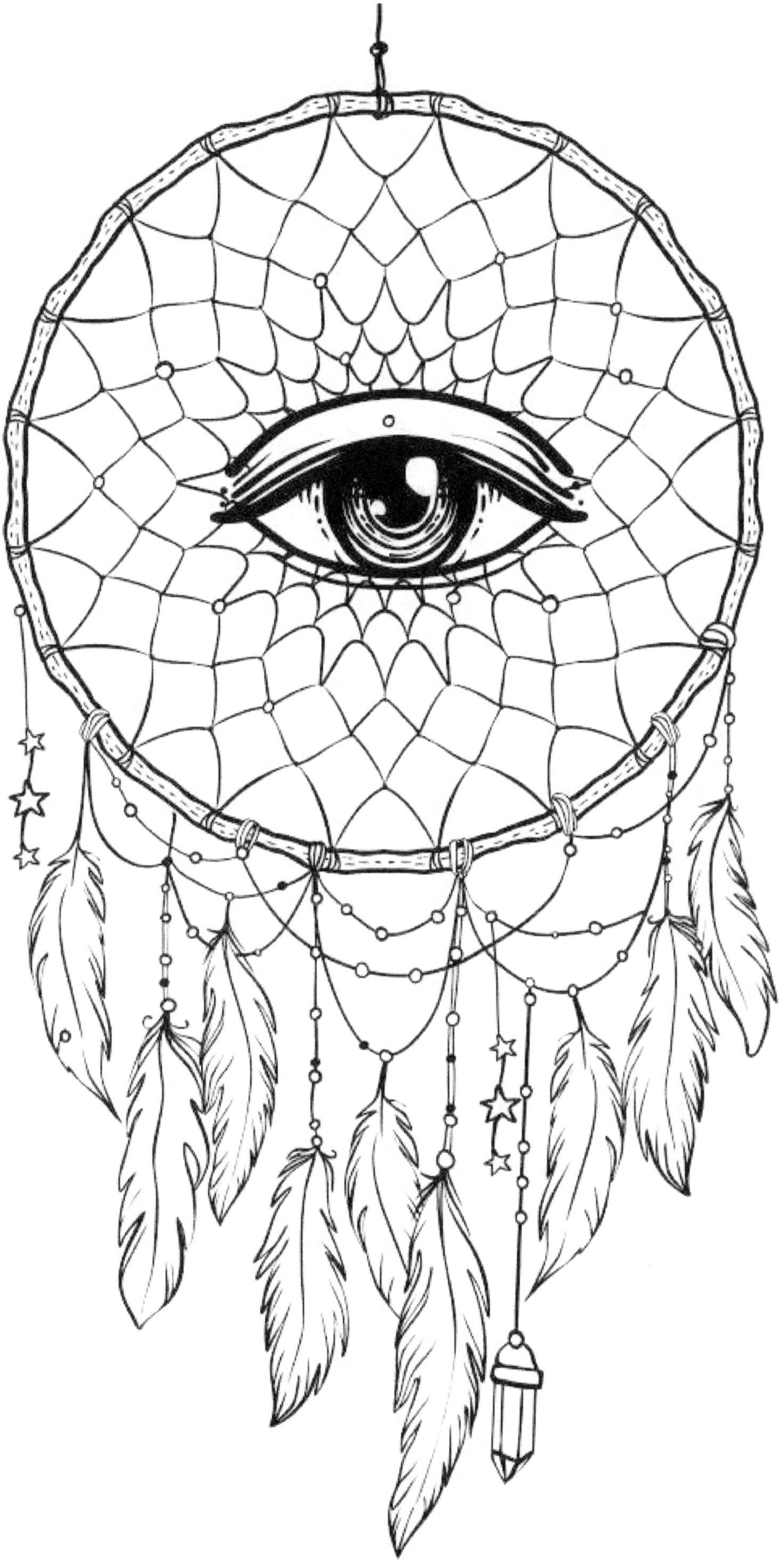

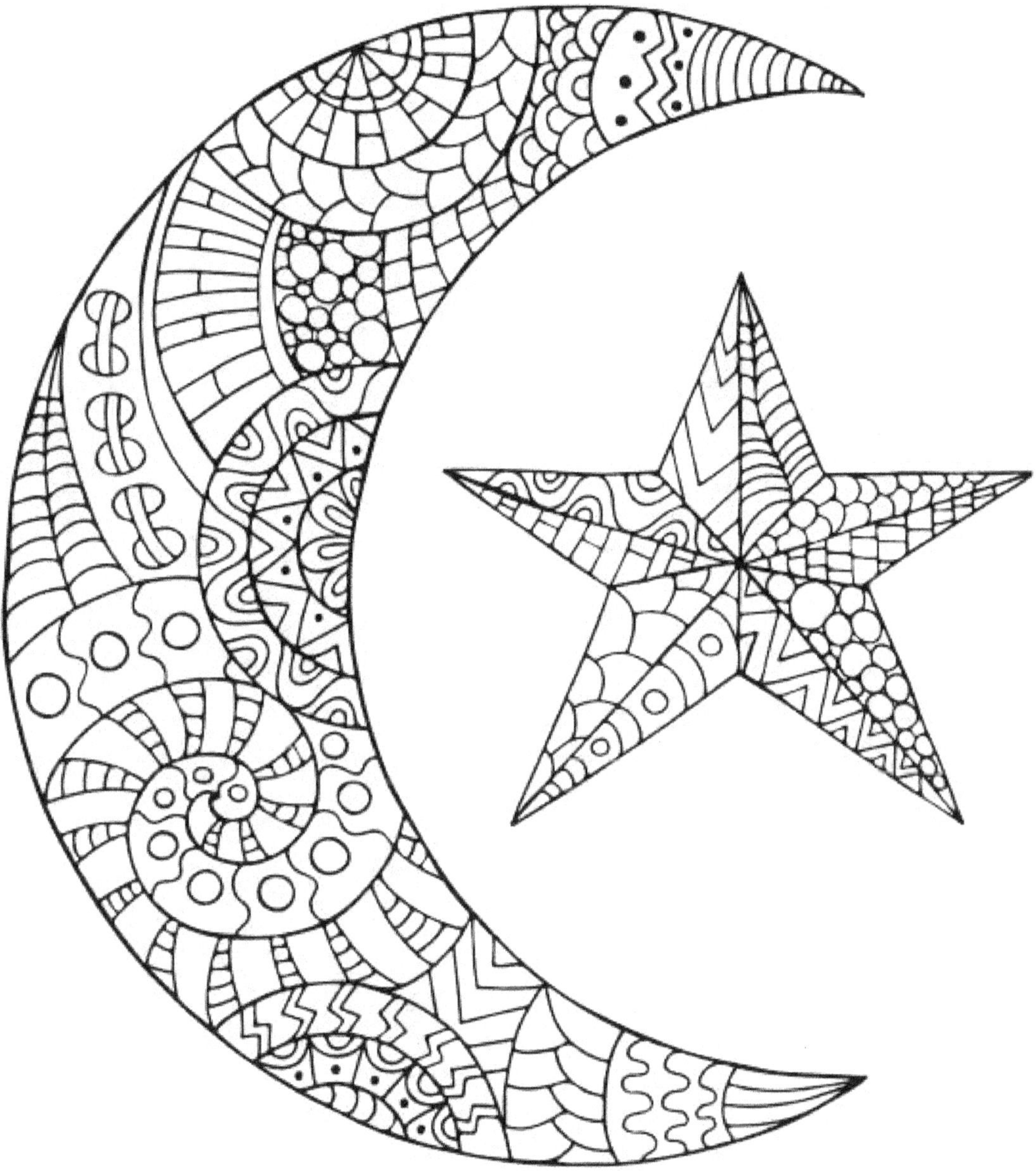

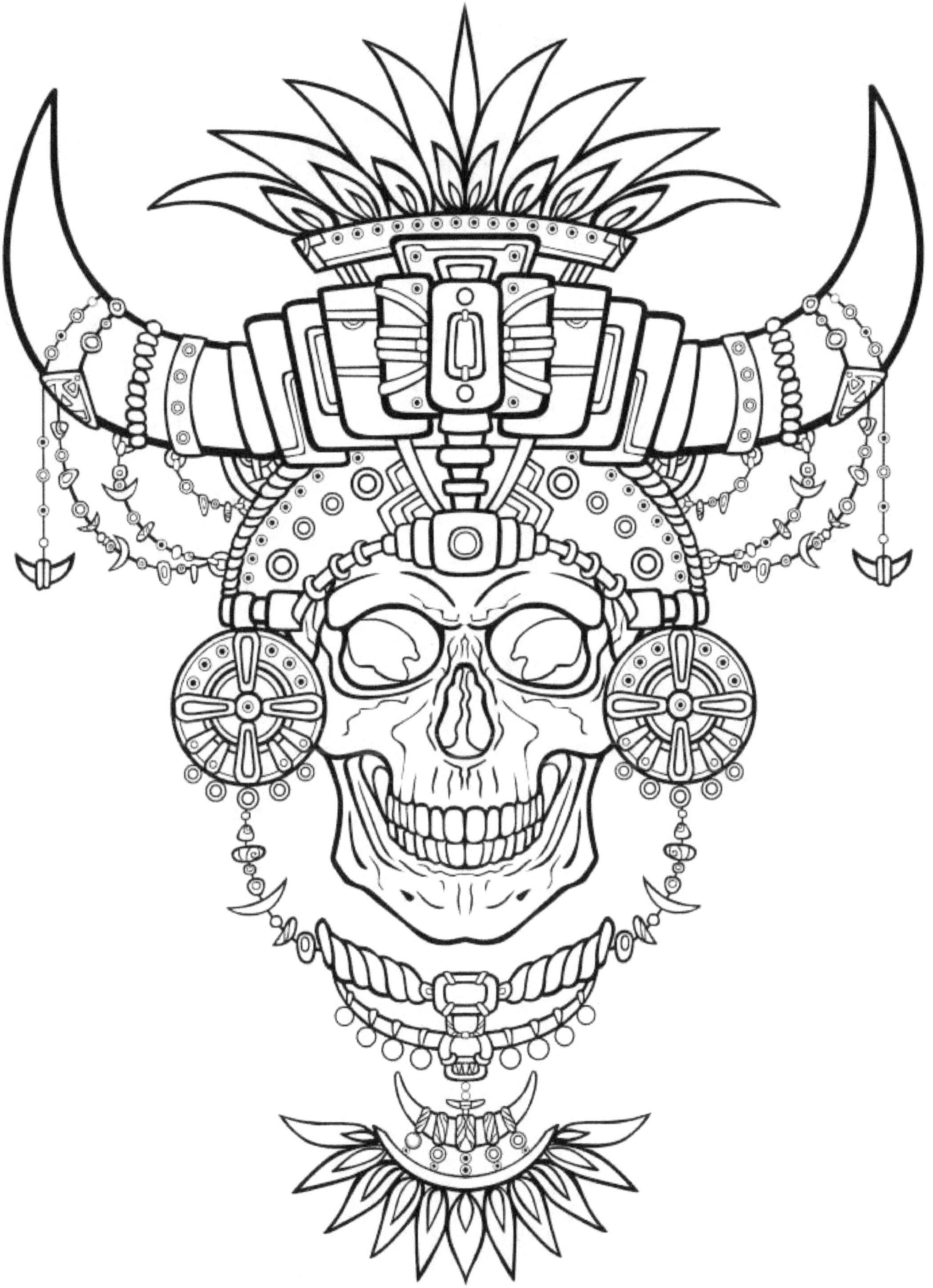

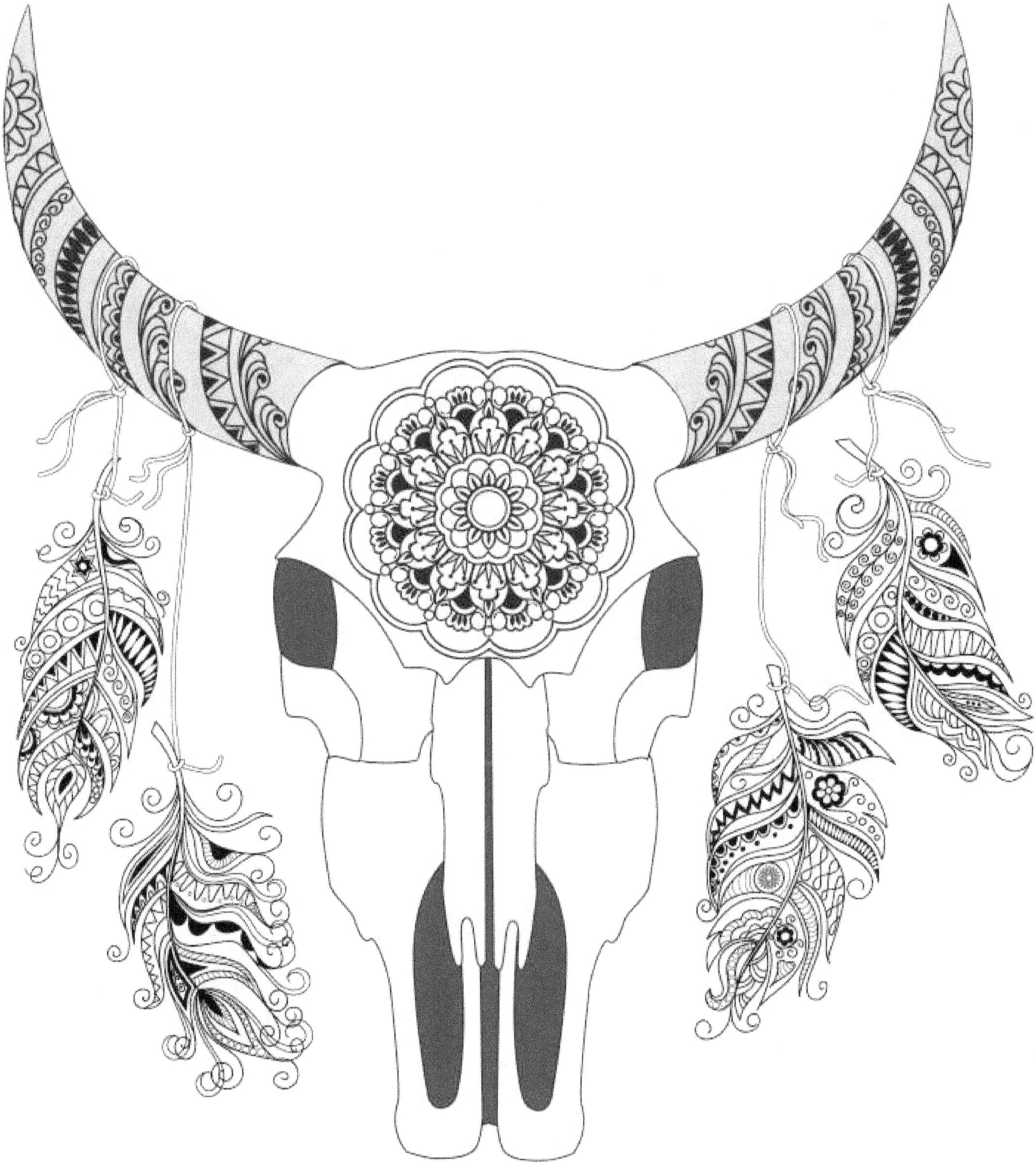

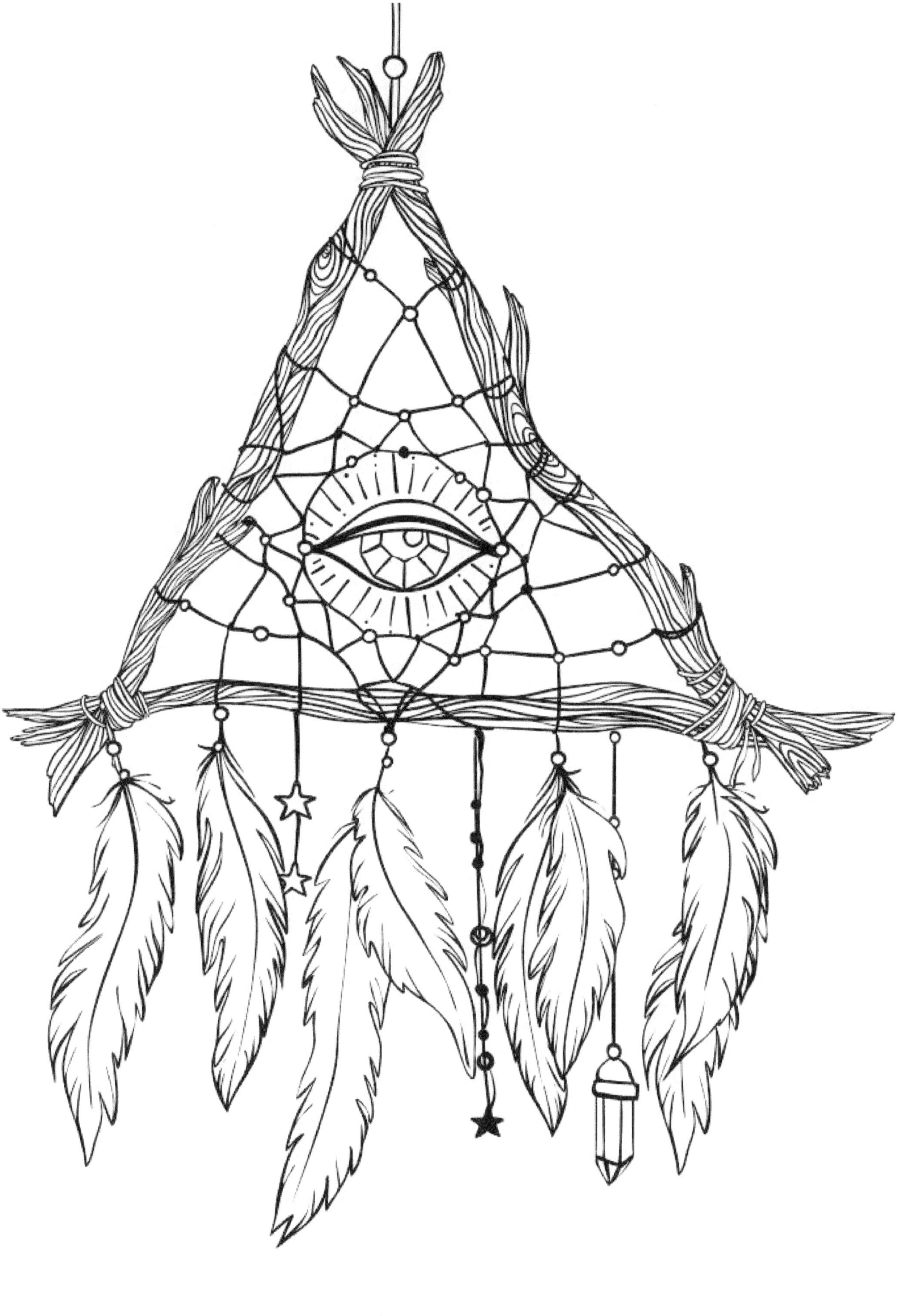

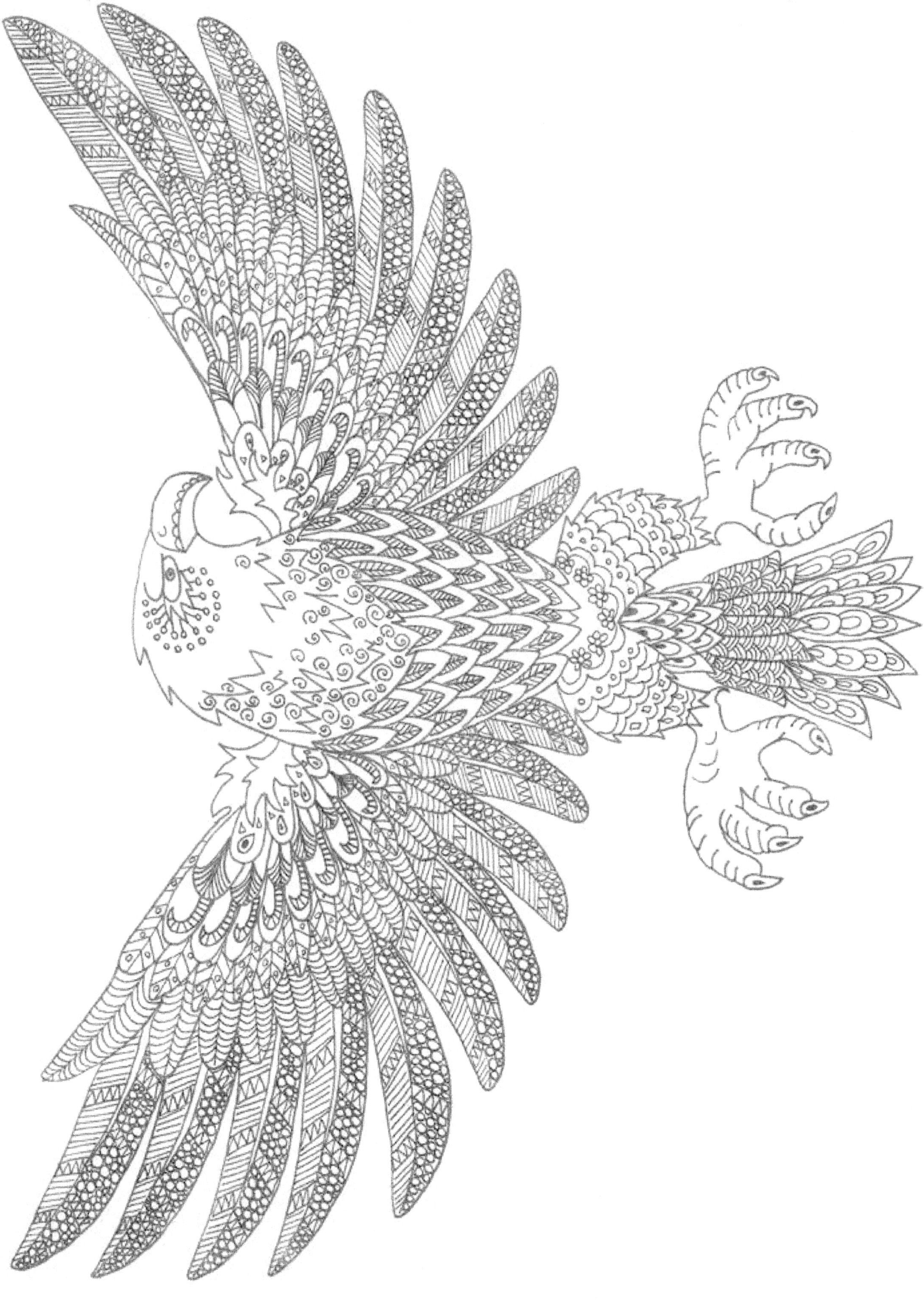

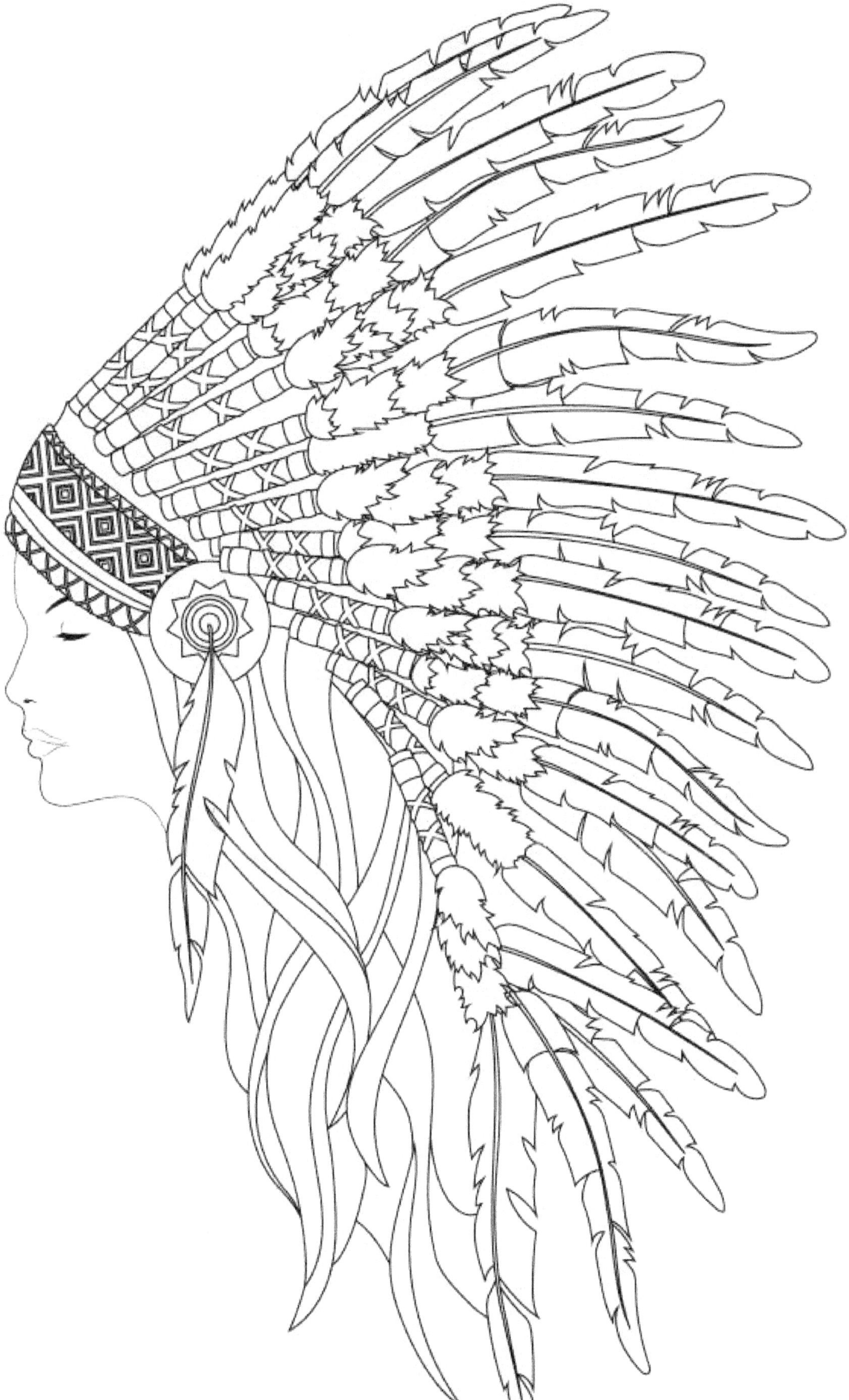

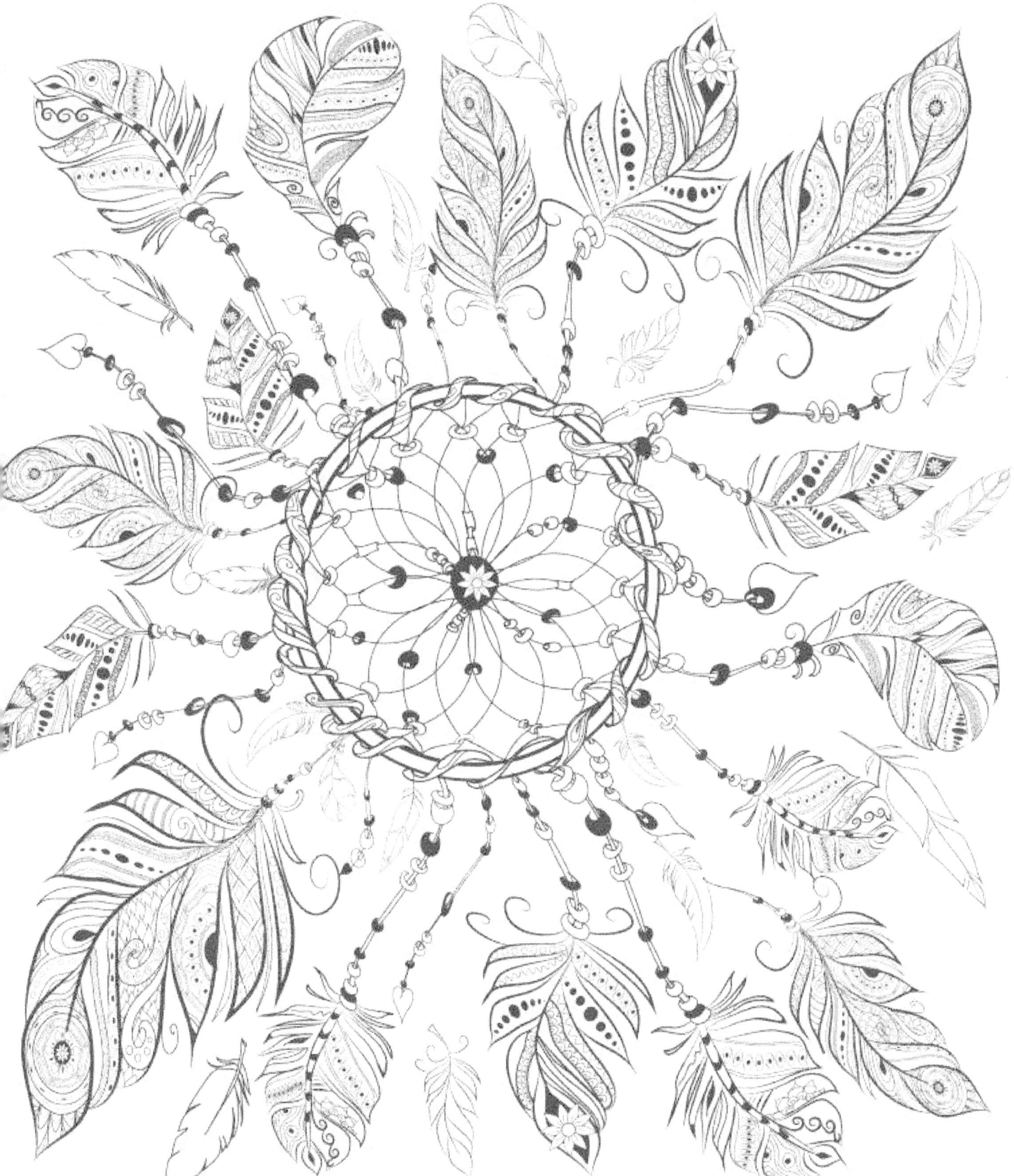

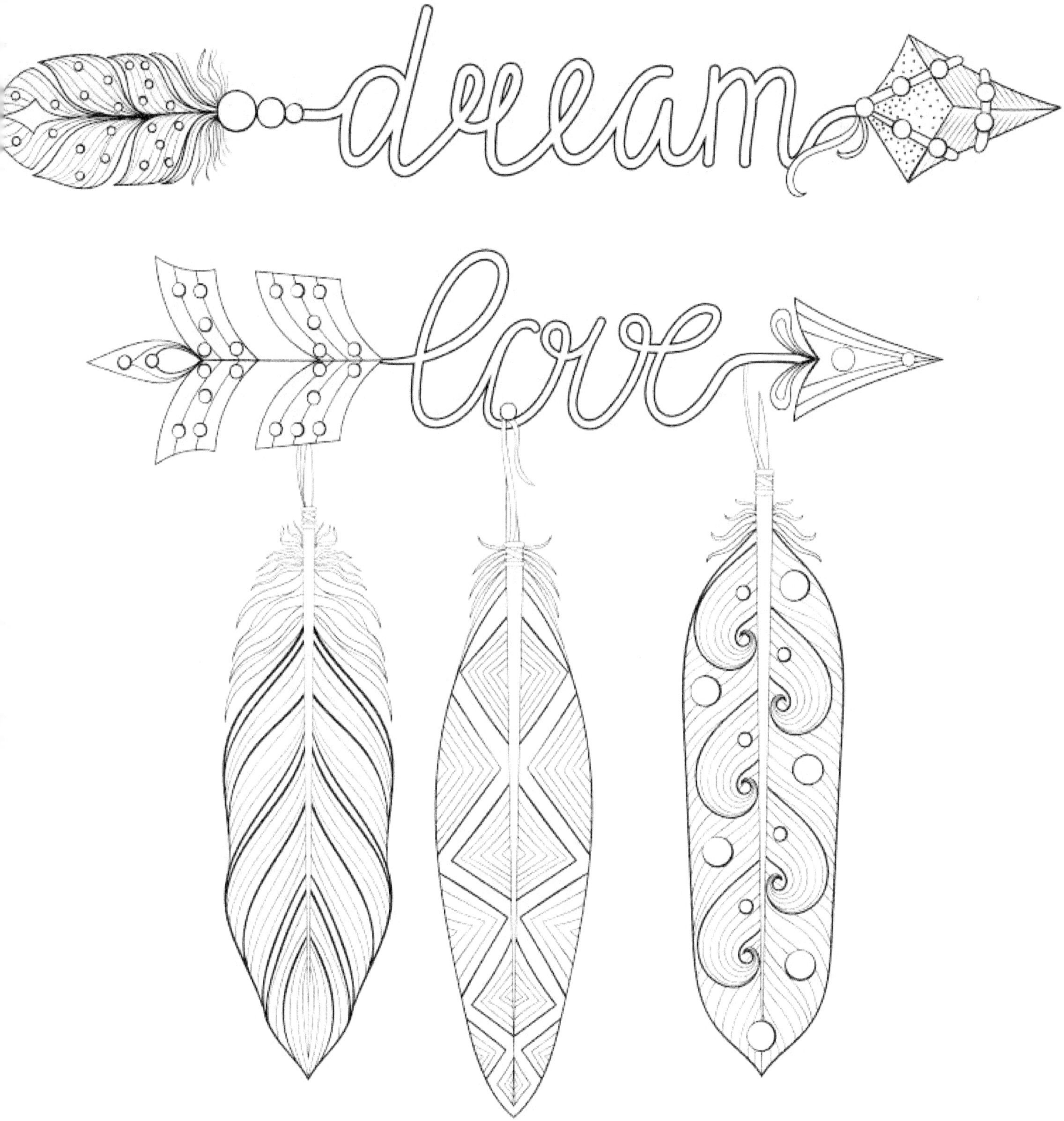
dream
love

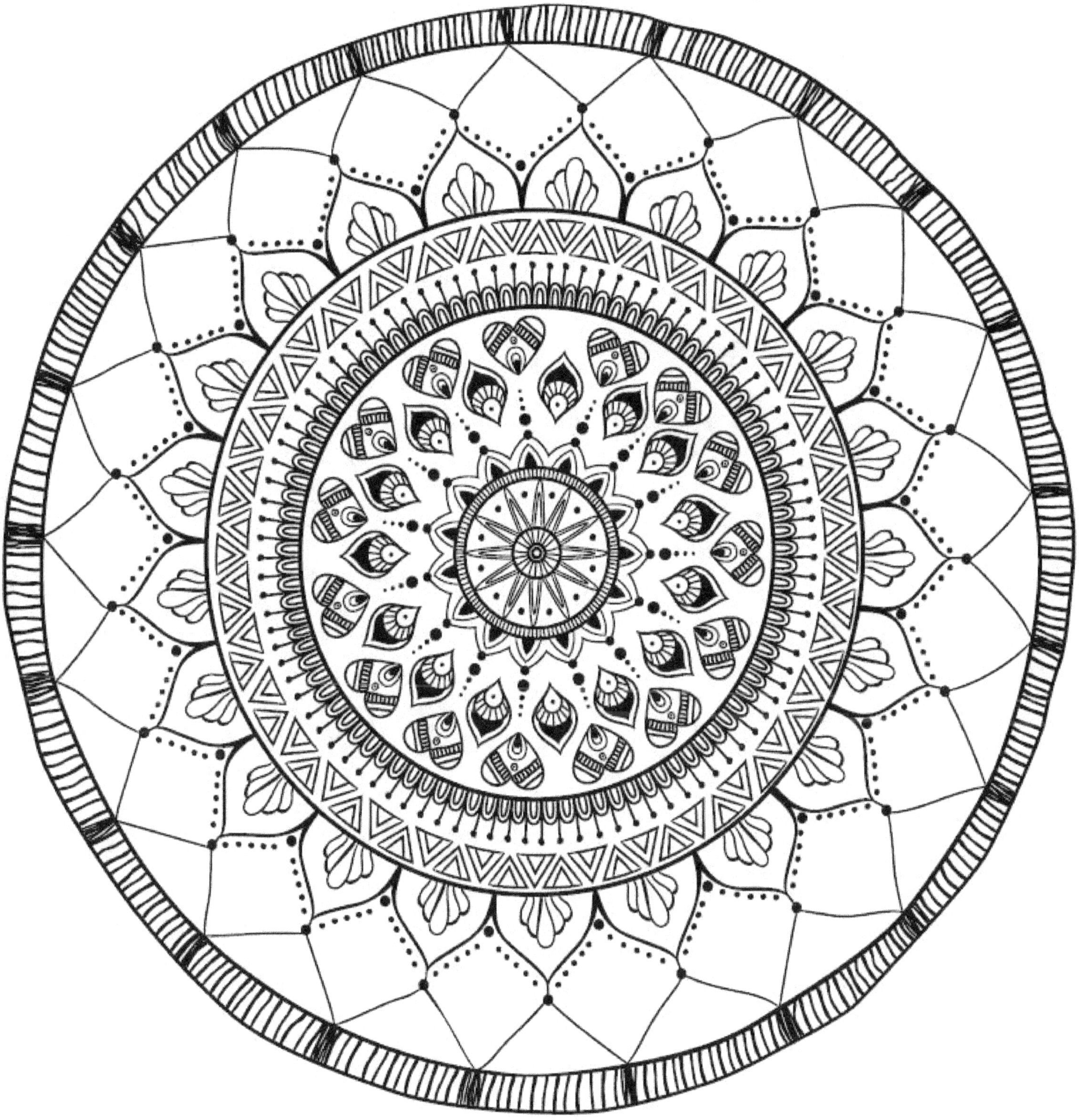

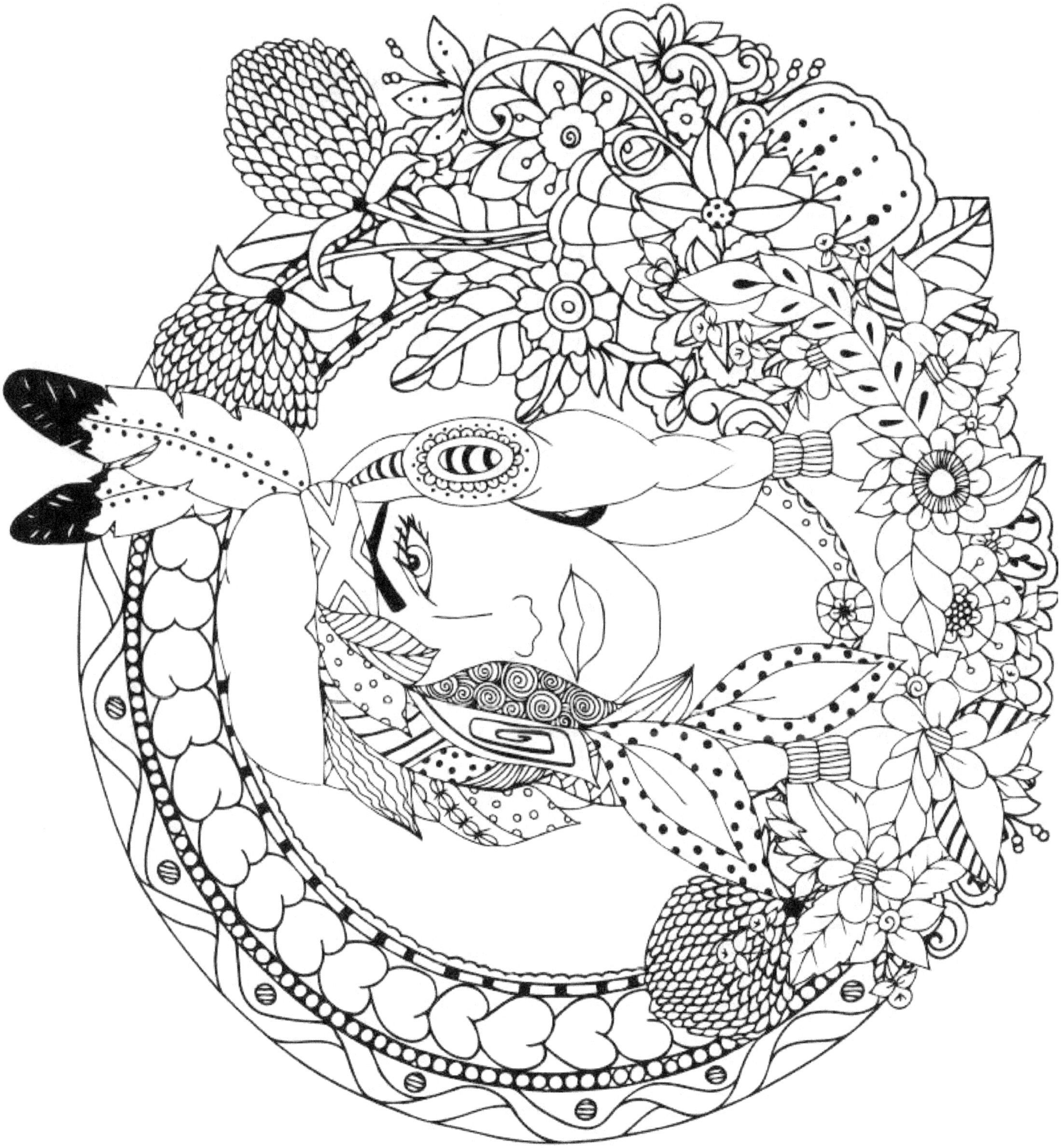

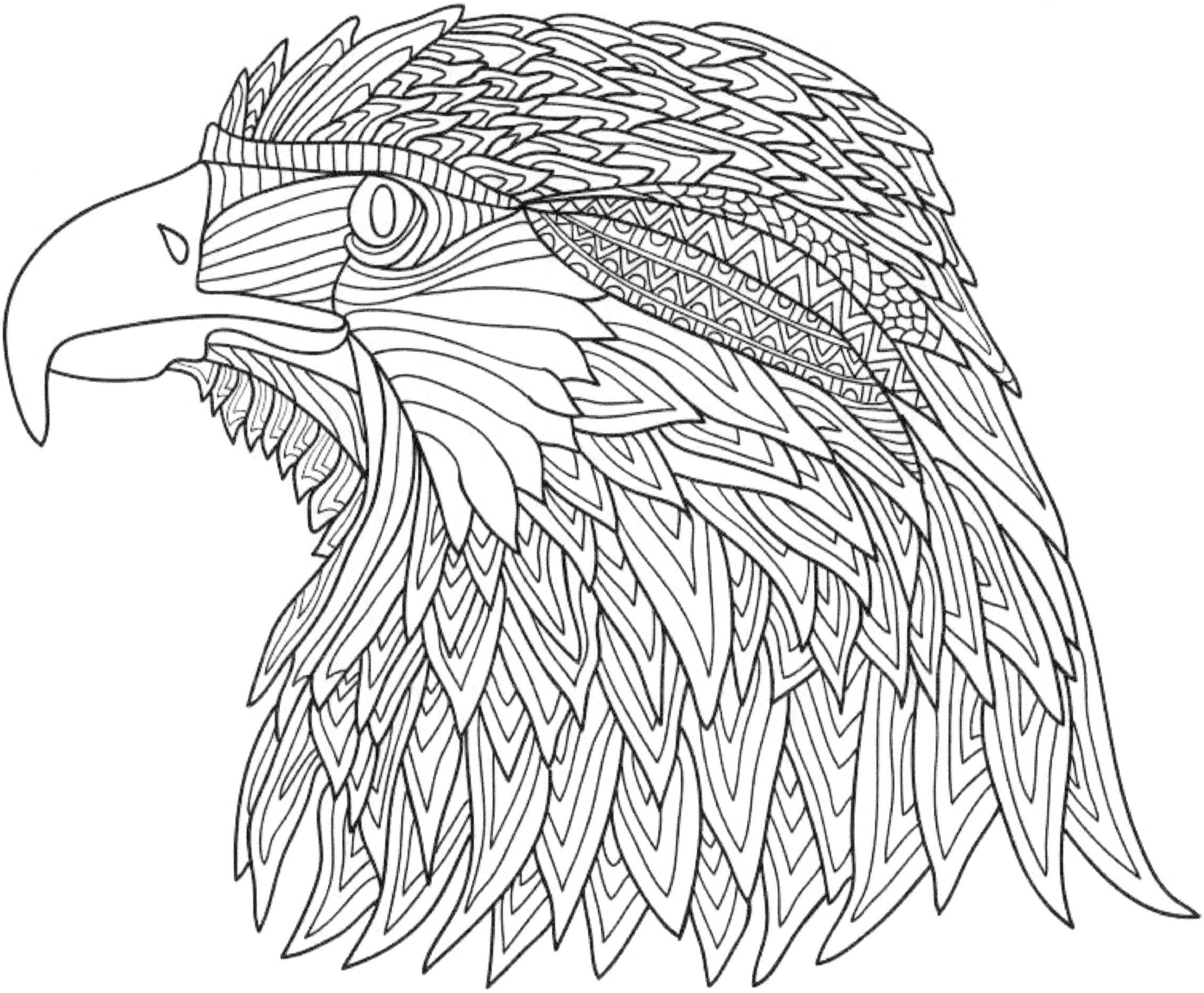

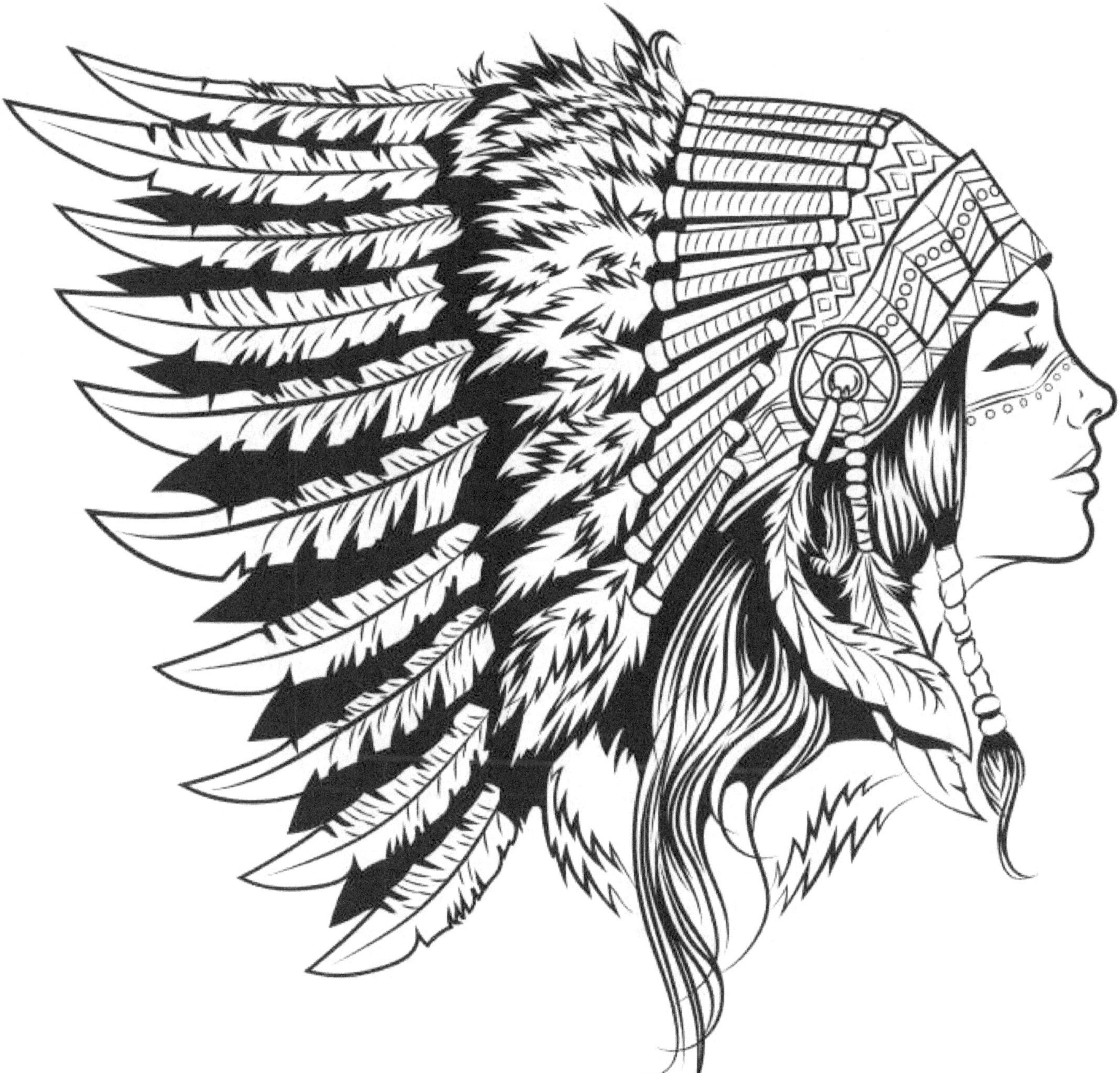

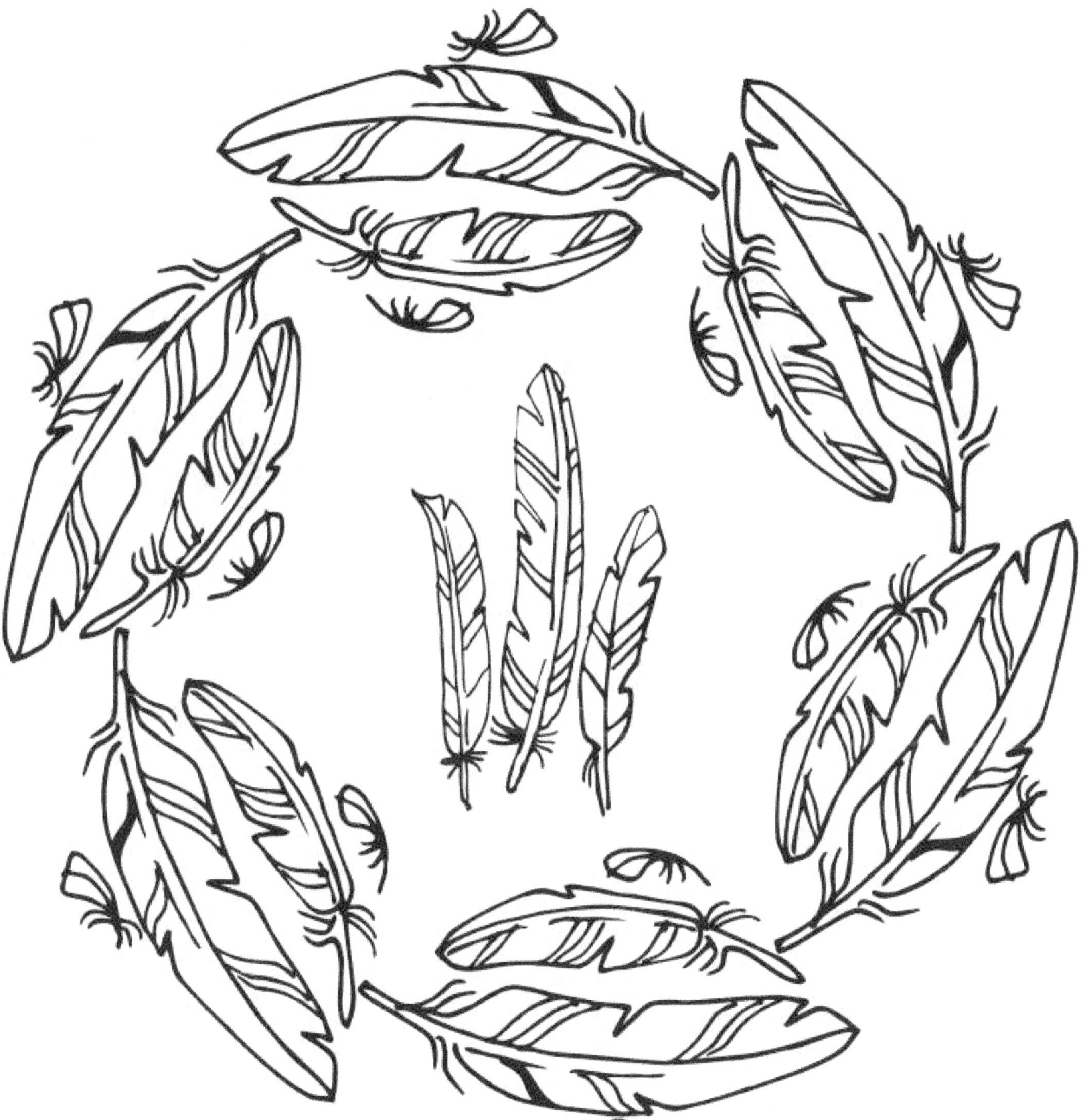

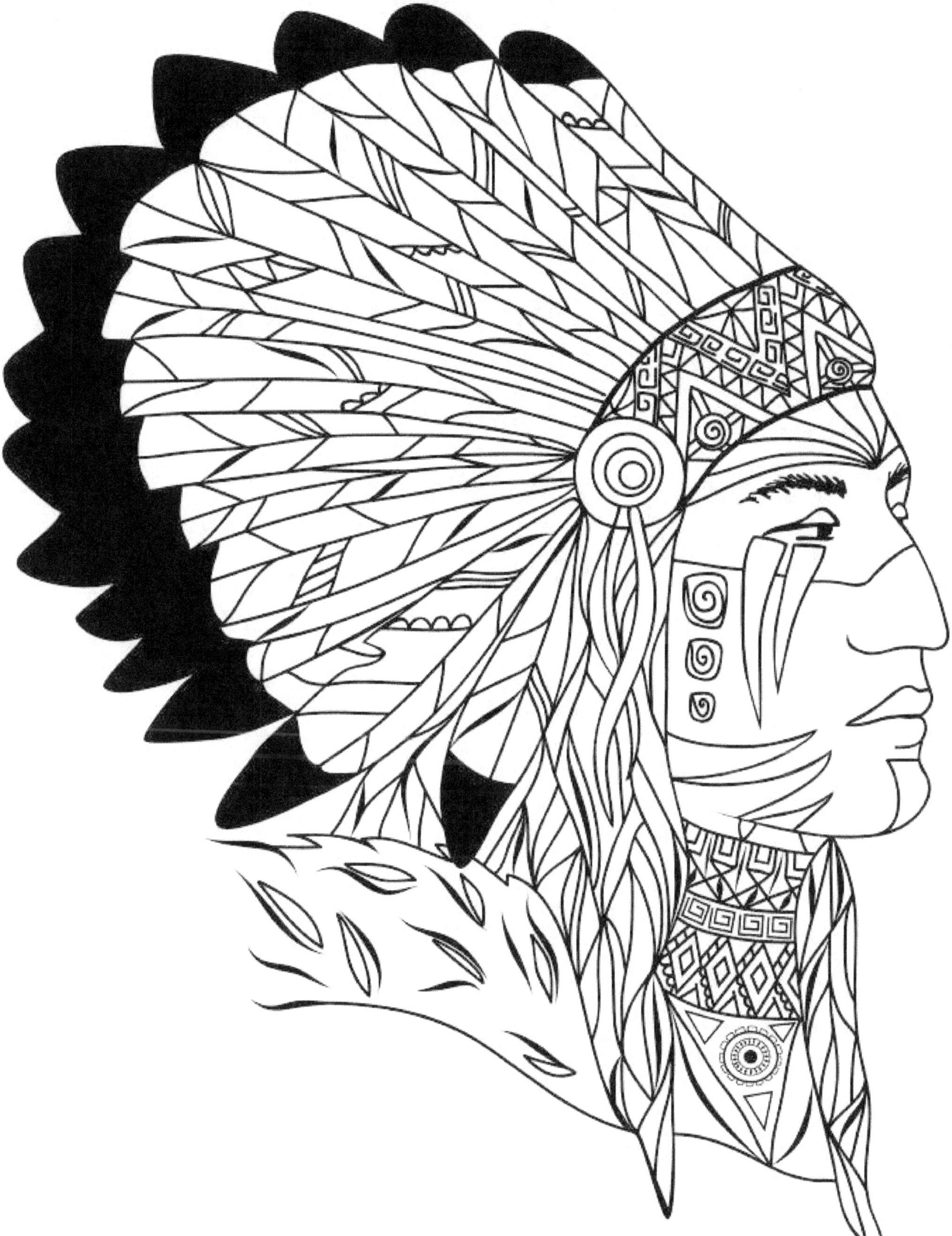

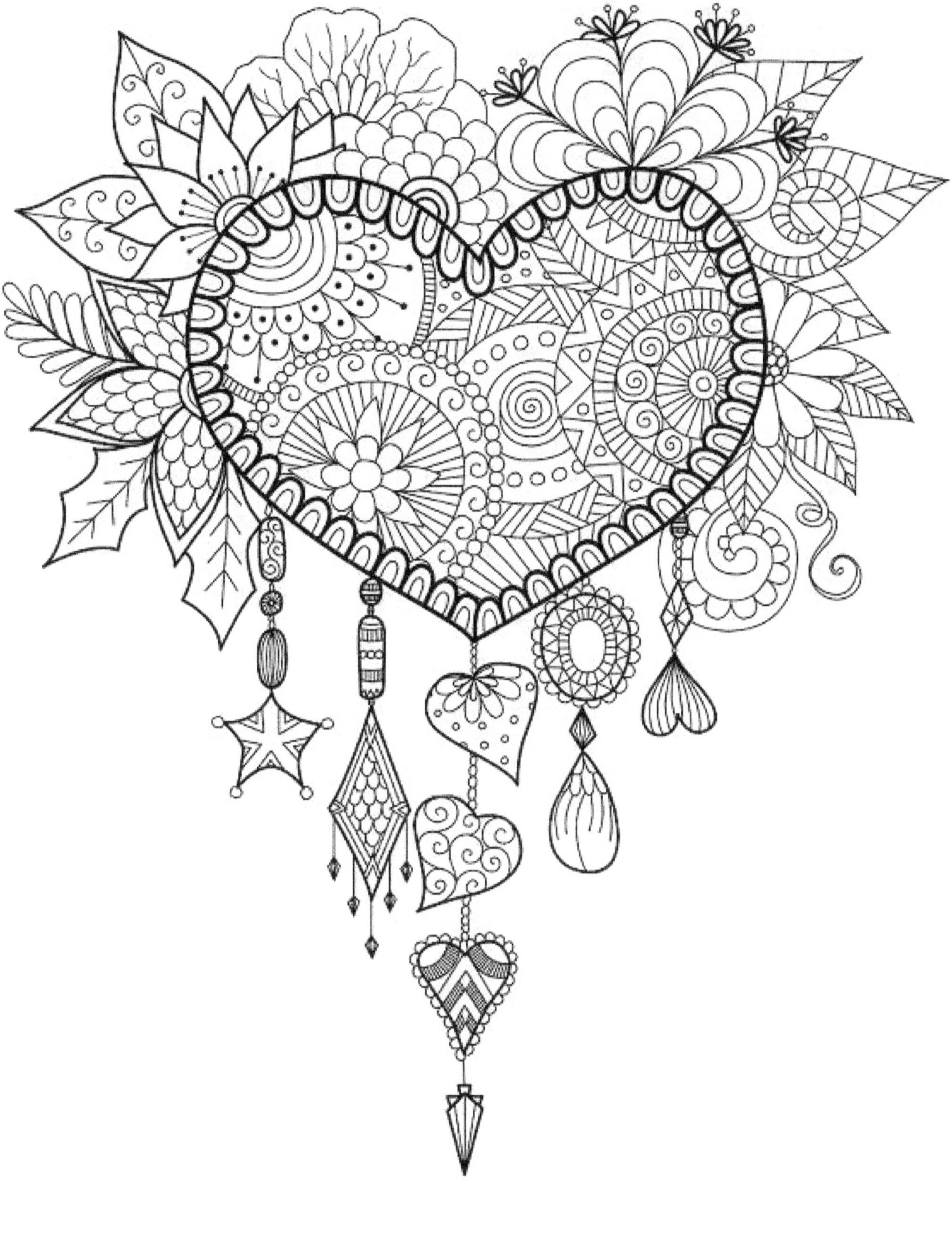

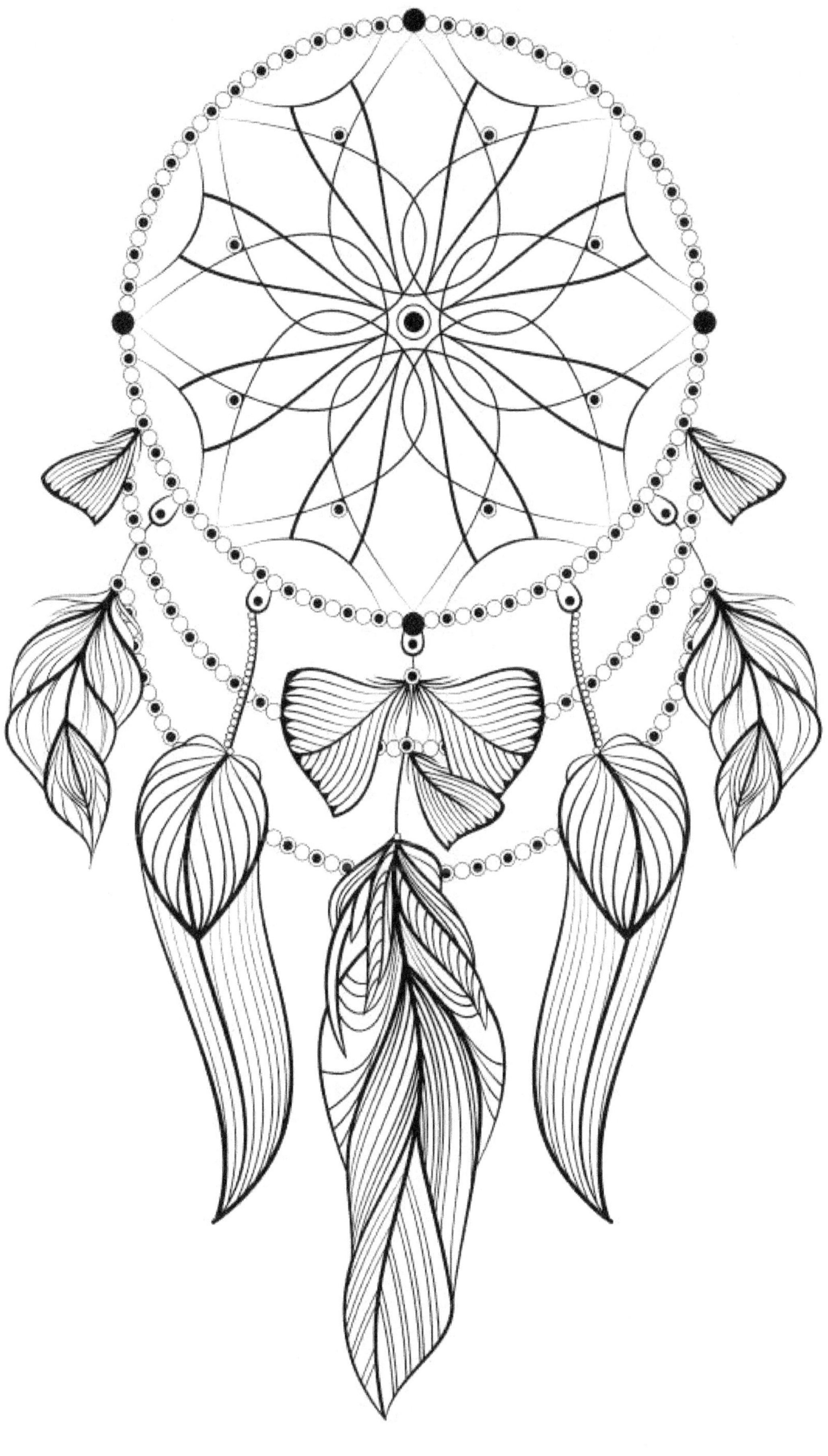

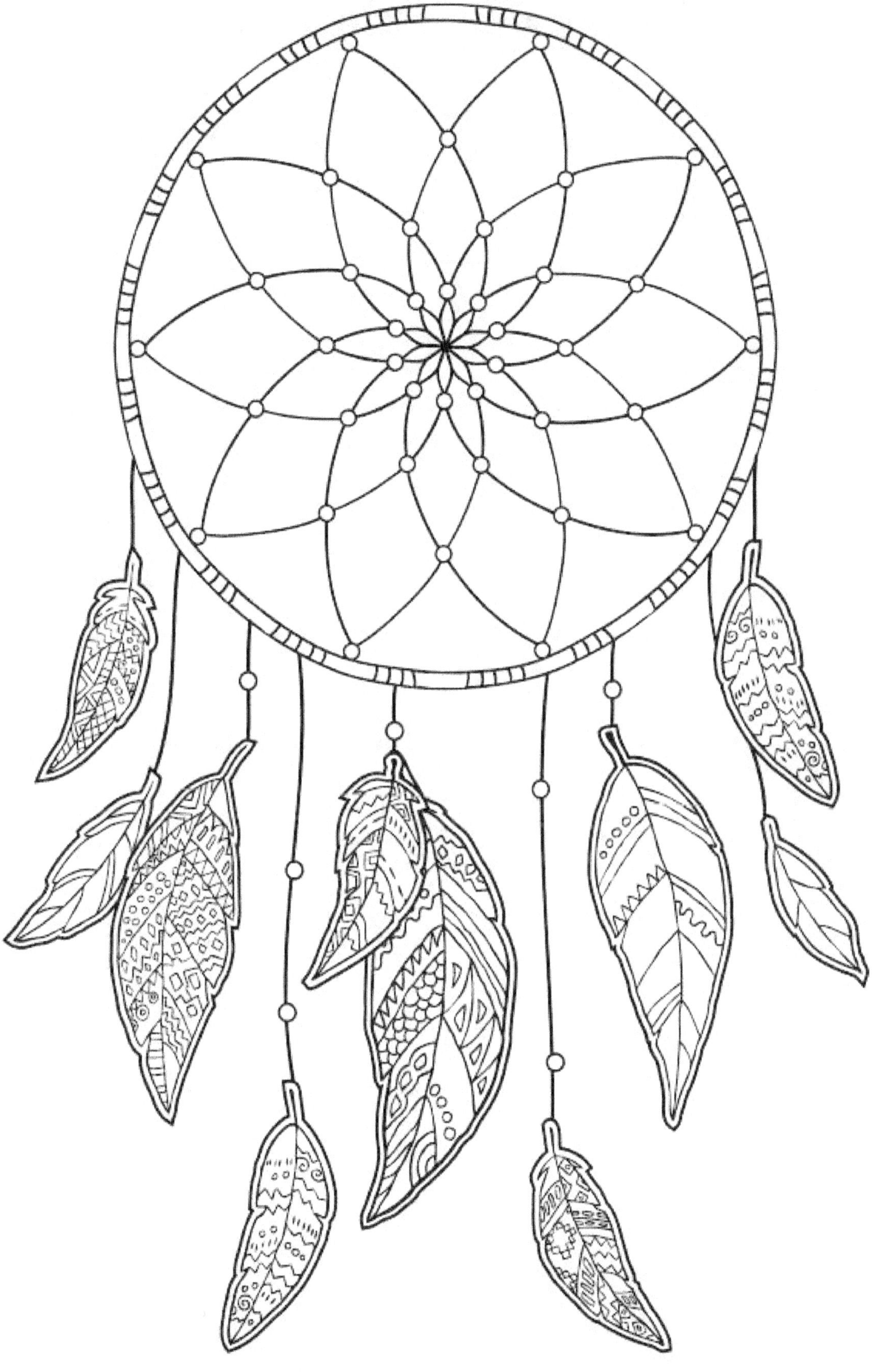

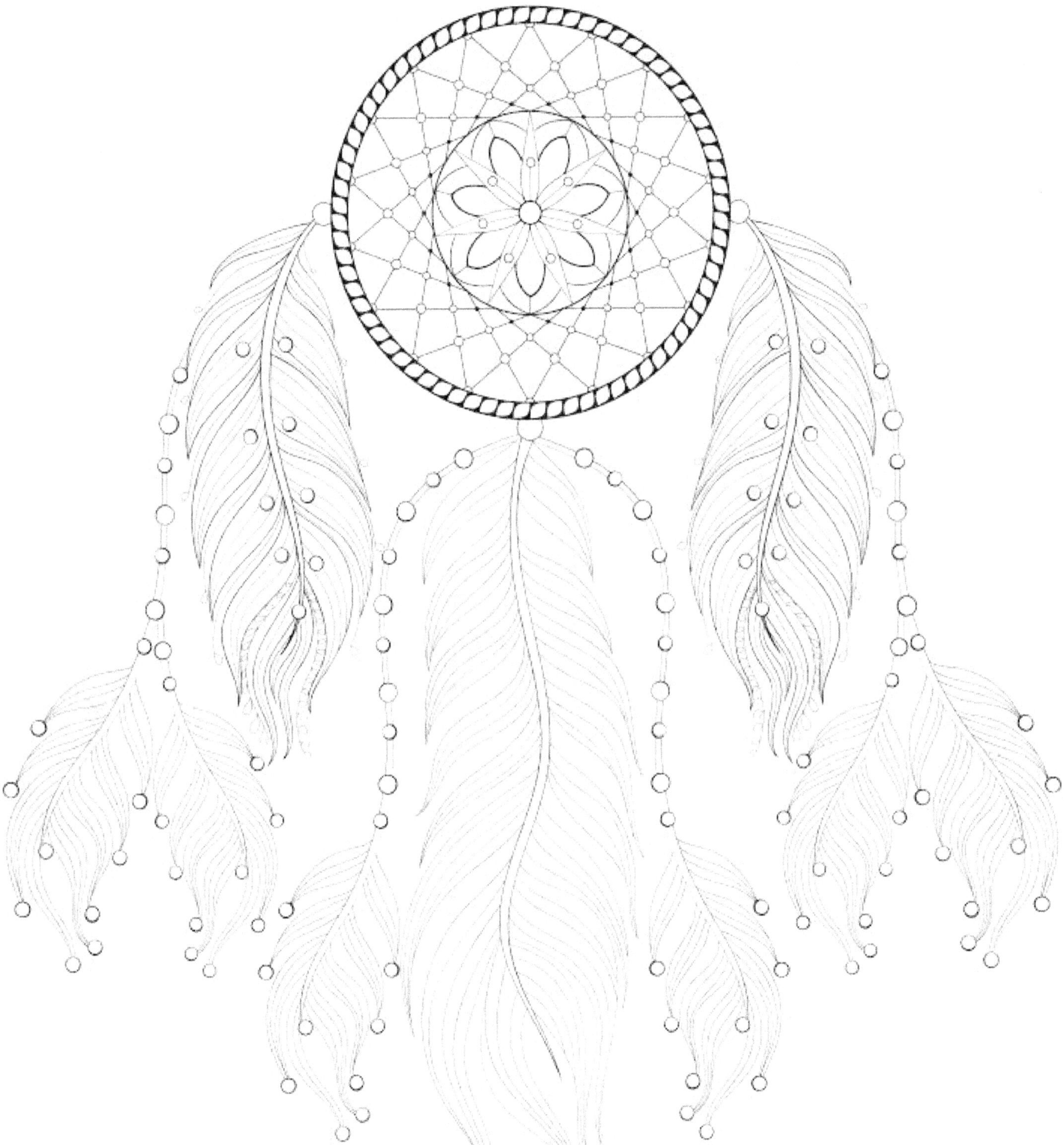

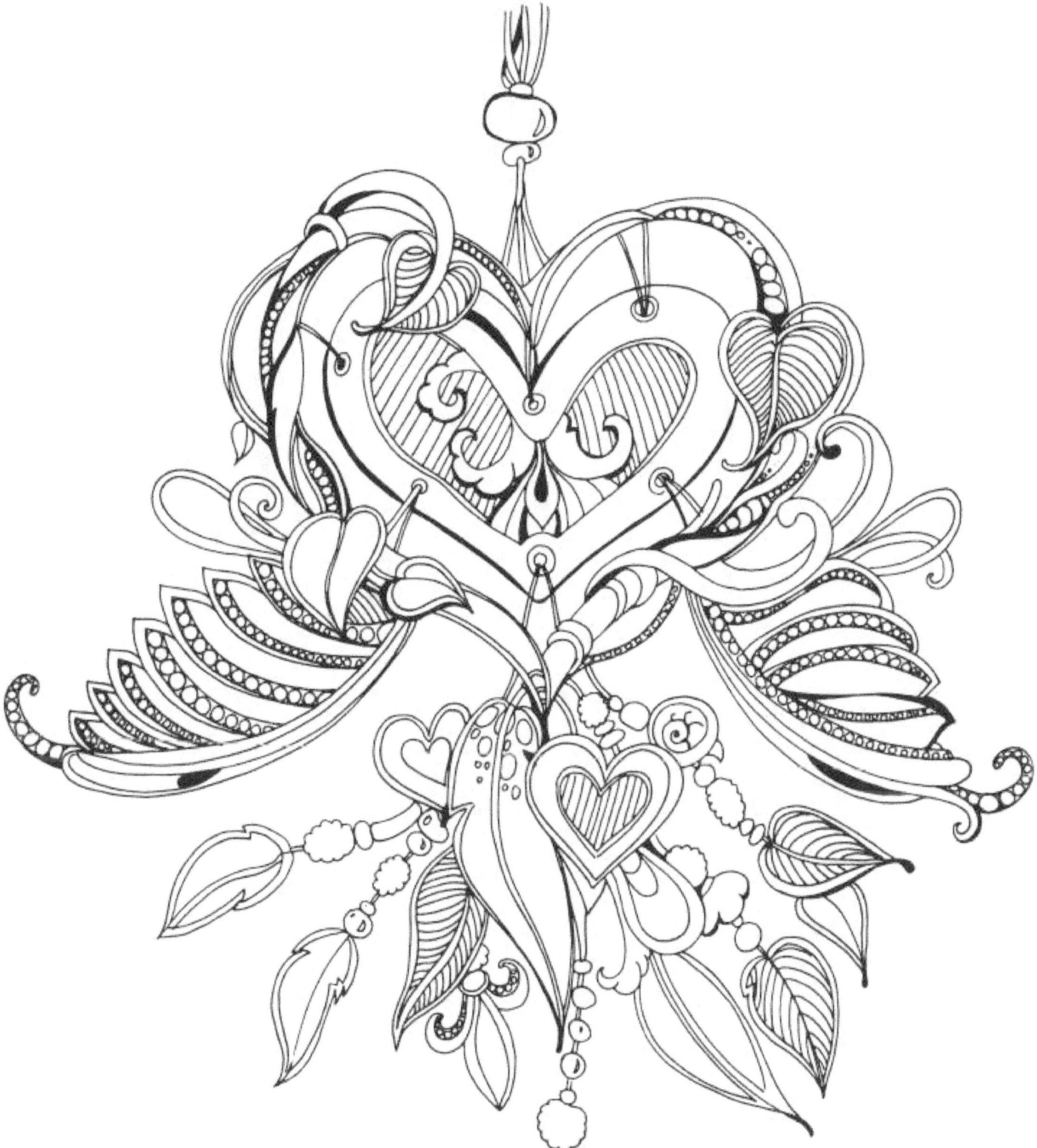

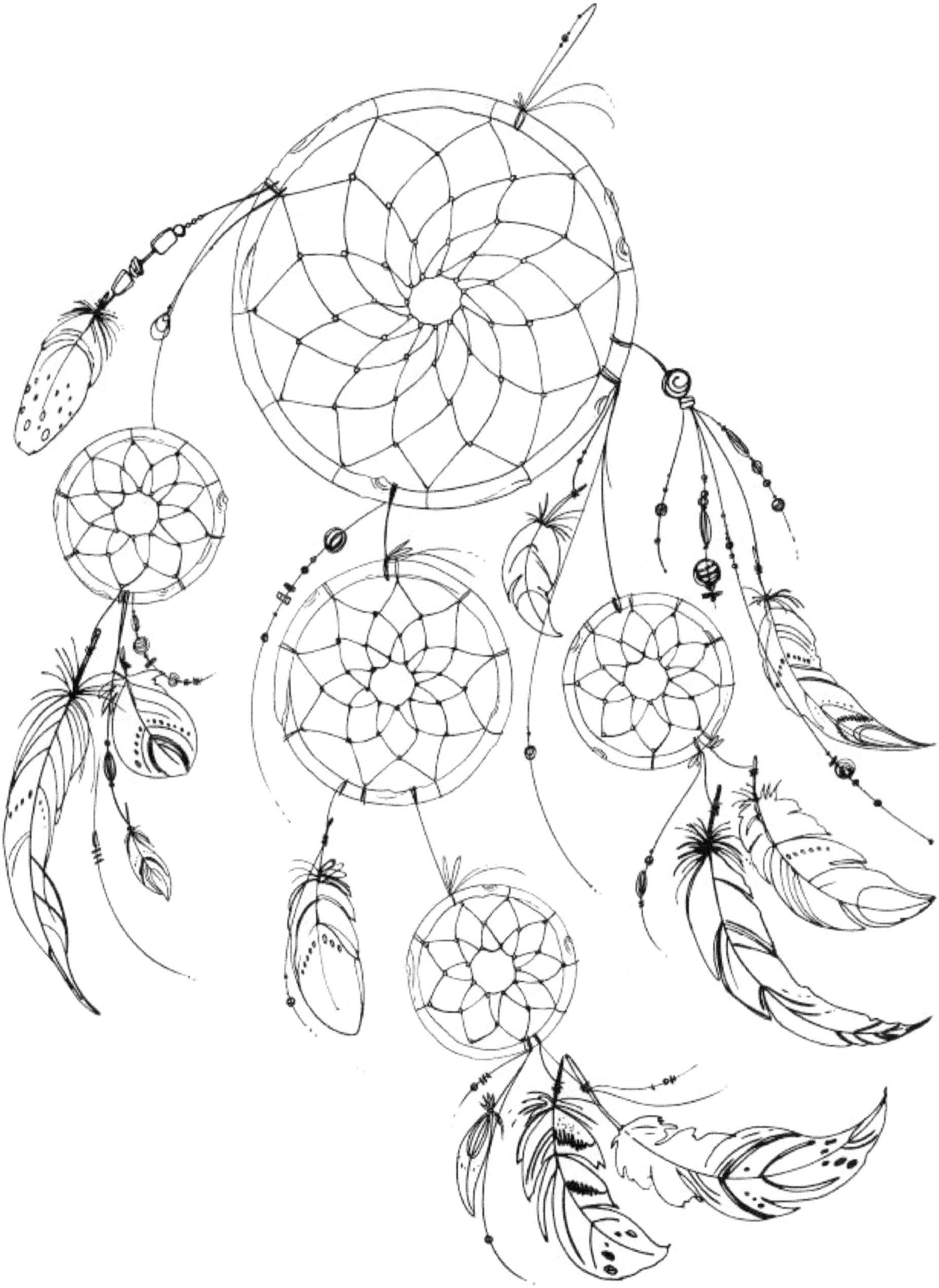

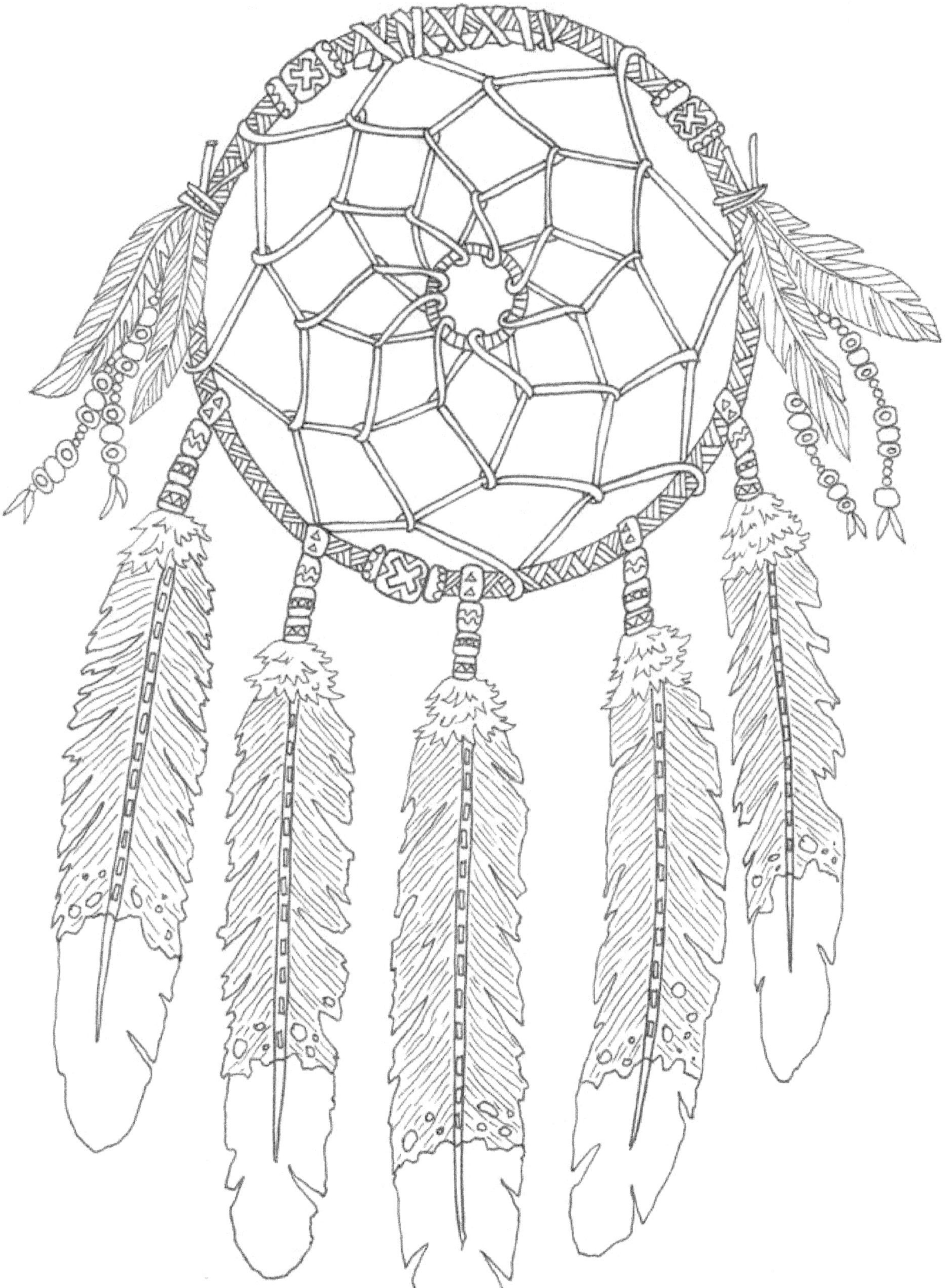

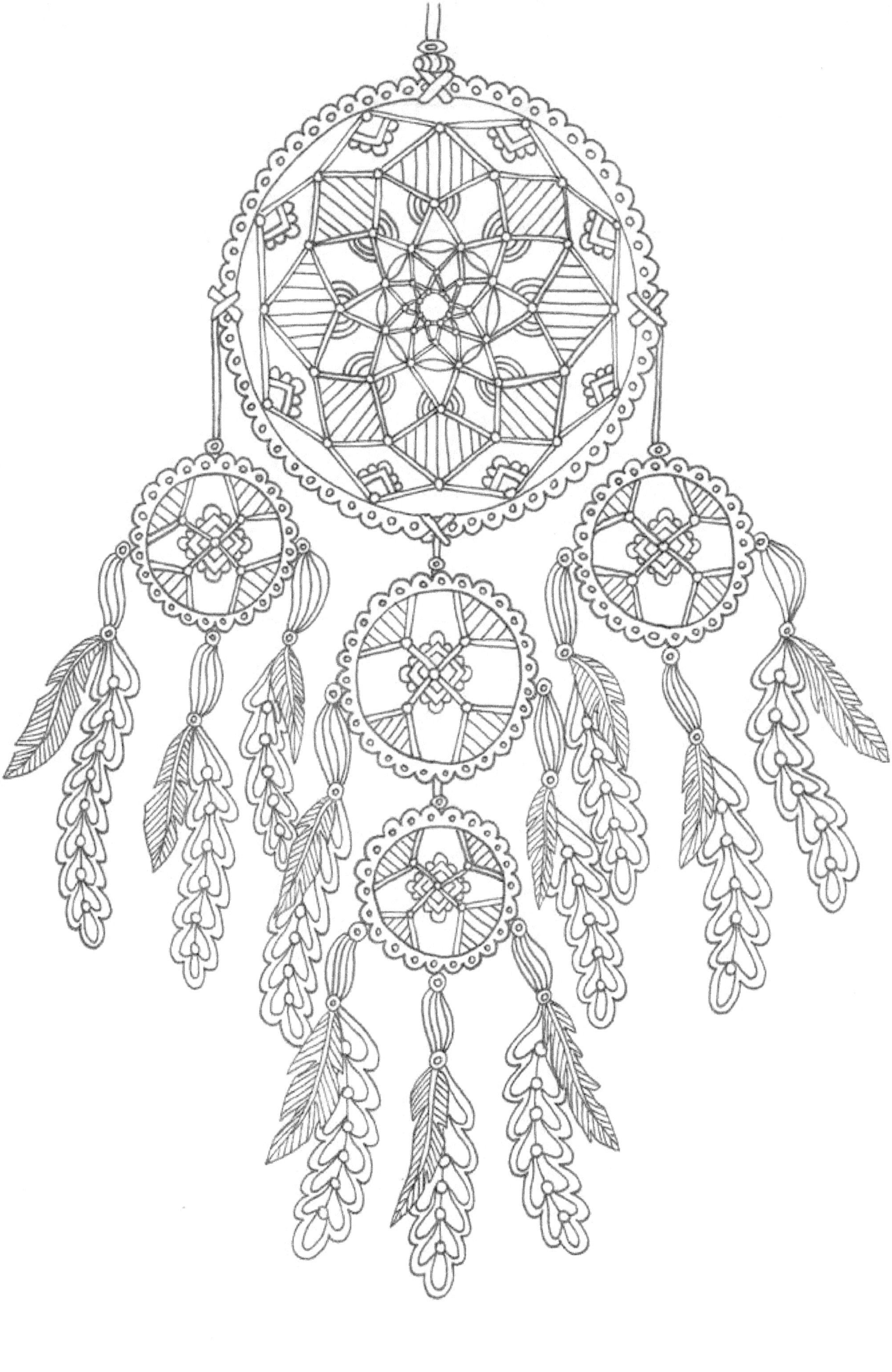

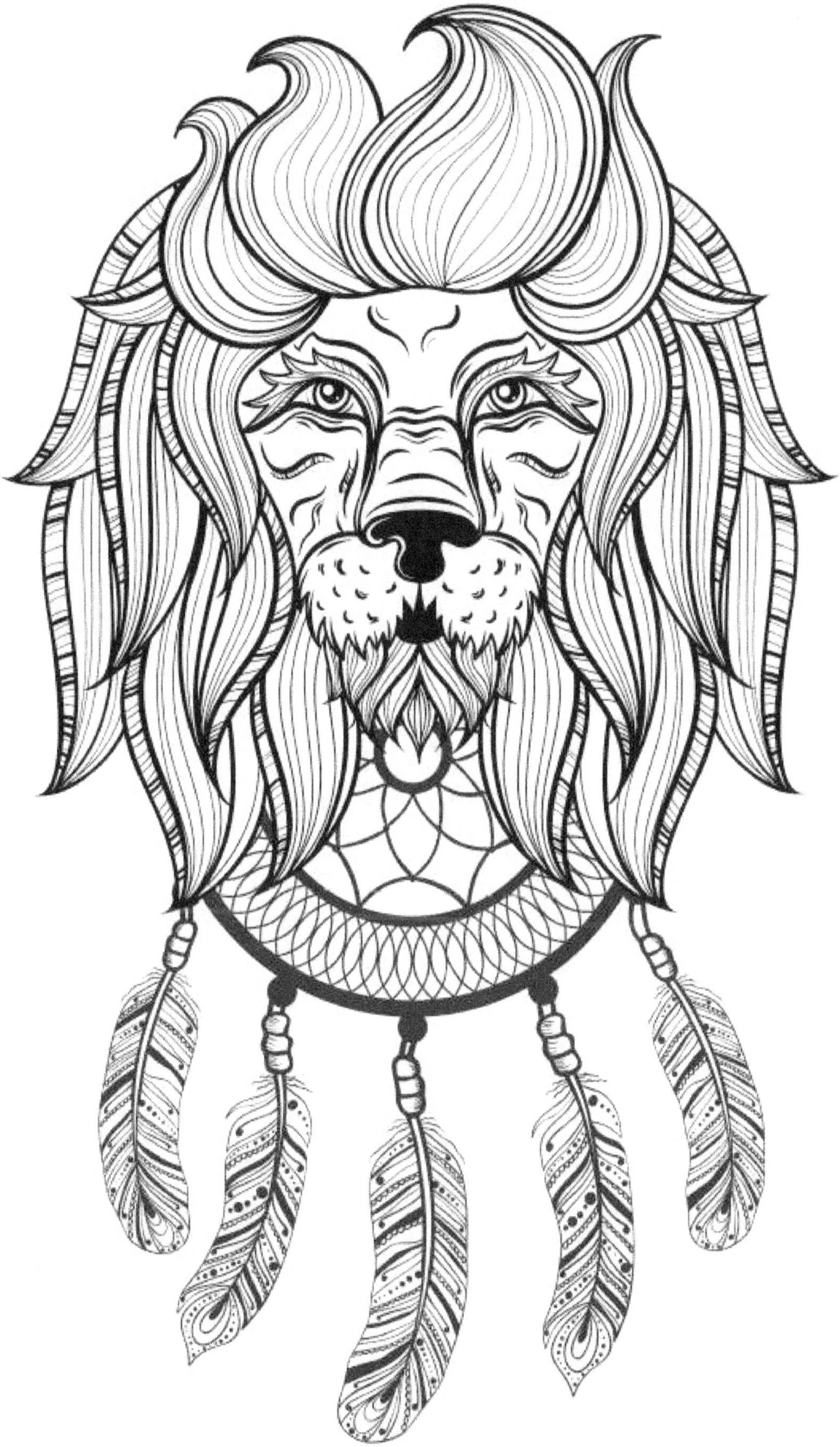

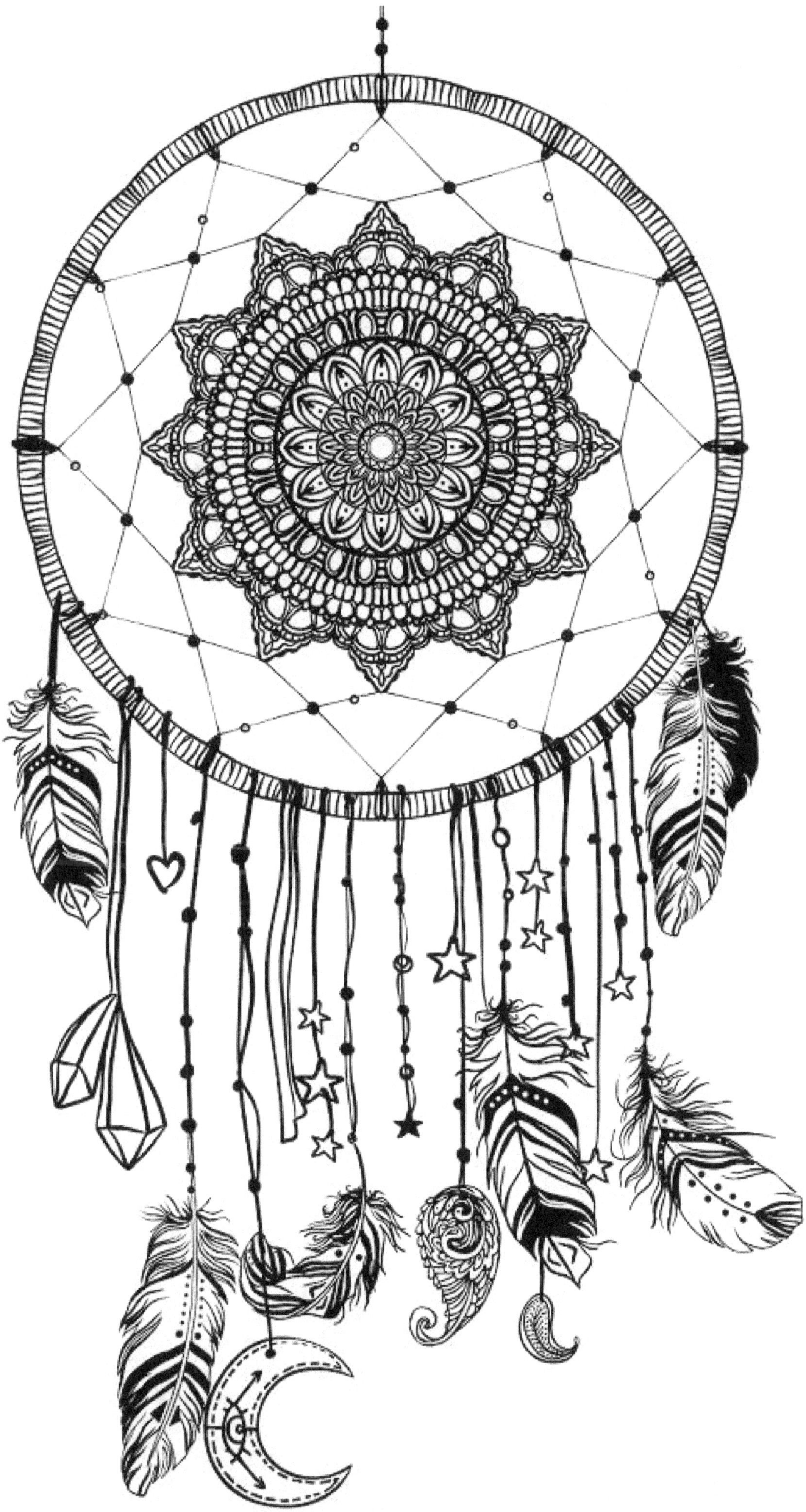

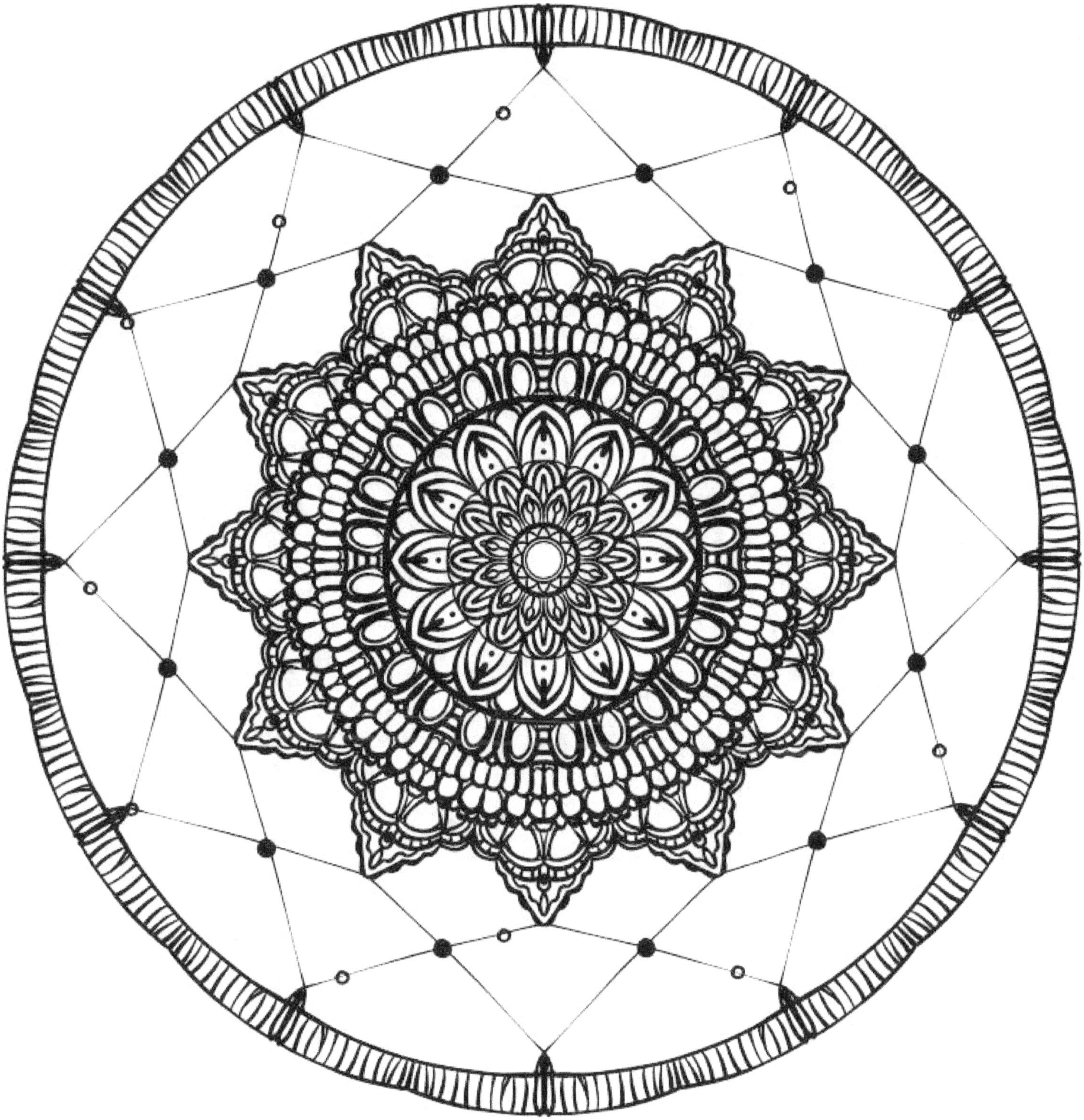

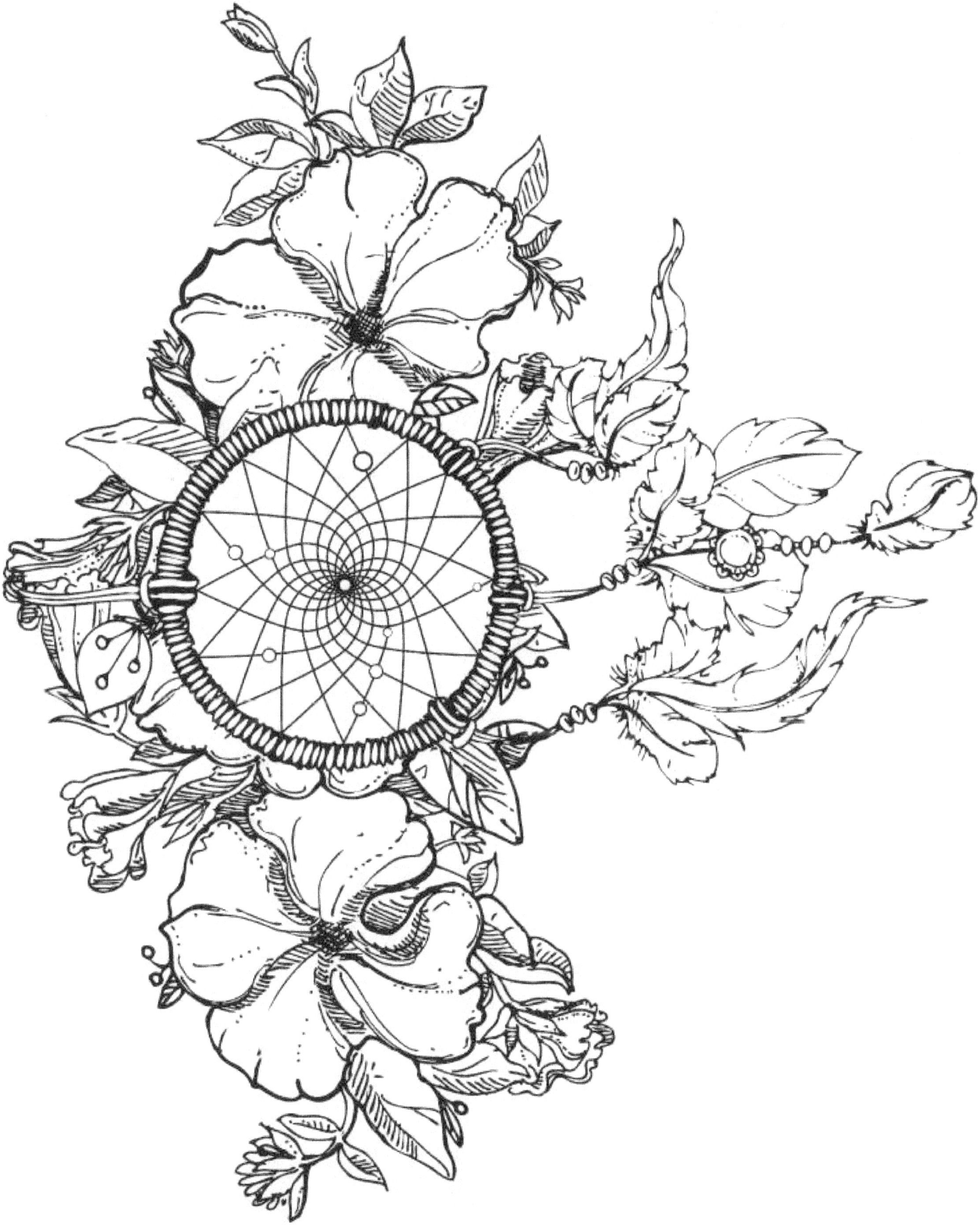

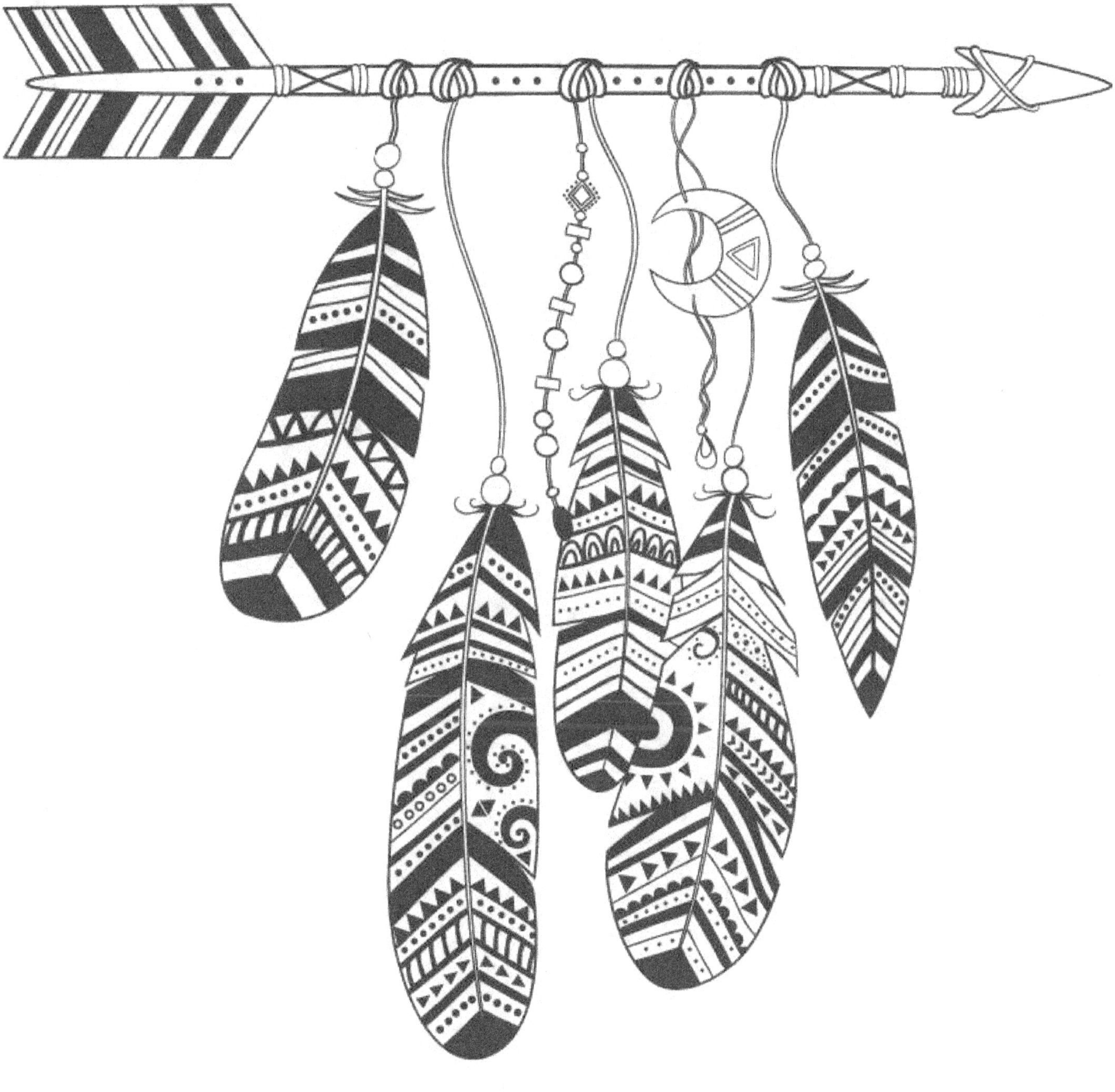

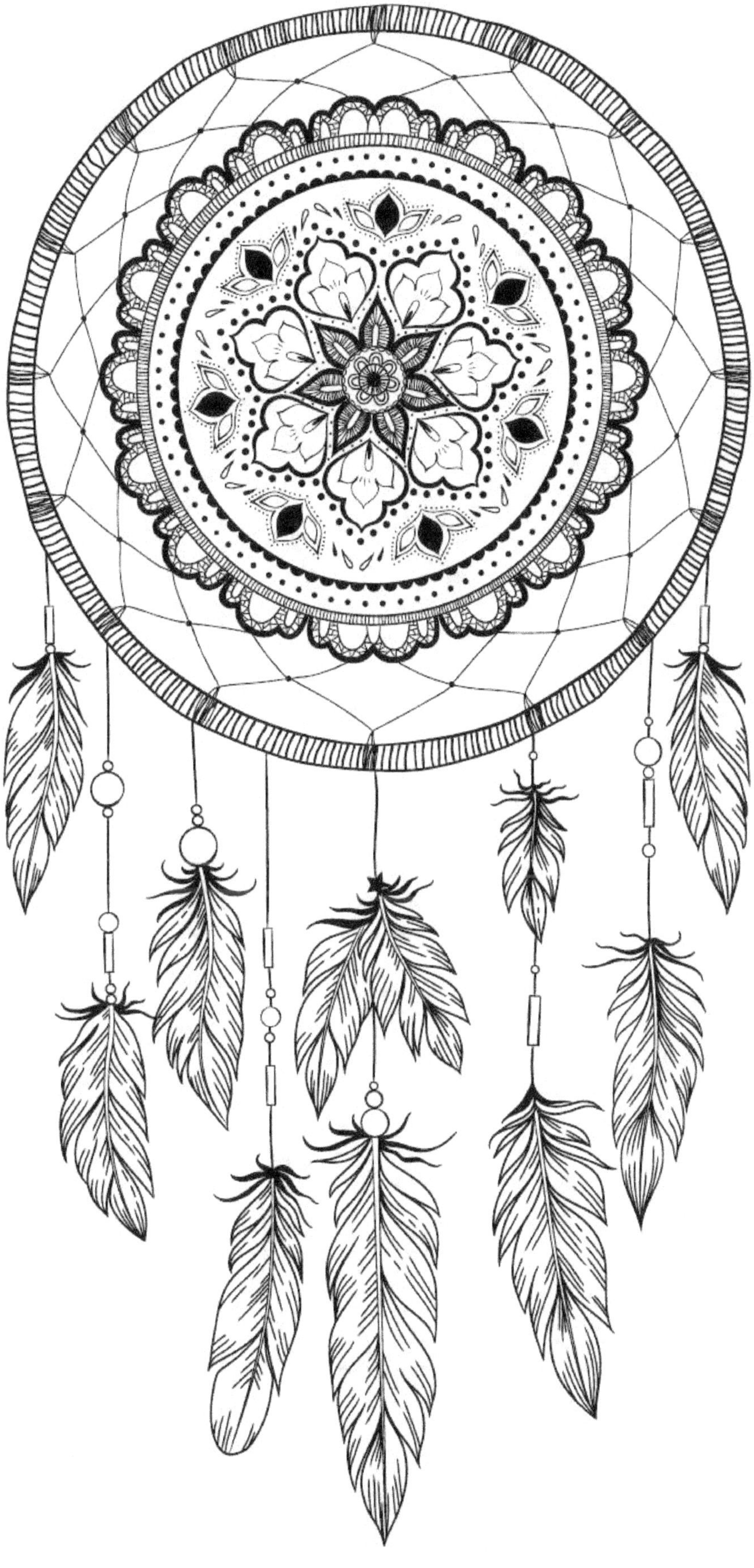

www.ingramcontent.com/pod-product-compliance
Lightning Source LLC
Chambersburg PA
CBHW081252180526
45170CB00007B/2401
* 9 7 8 1 5 4 7 0 1 9 3 7 3 *